W9-AUI-926

248.843
Bre

BECOMING A WOMAN
TRANSFORMED BY

The COLORS
of HIS LOVE

DEE BRESTIN &
KATHY TROCCOLI

6245

MEDIA CENTER (LIBRARY)
Pleasant Valley Baptist Church
Amarillo, Texas 79108

W PUBLISHING GROUP™
www.wpublishinggroup.com

A Division of Thomas Nelson, Inc.
www.ThomasNelson.com

Copyright © 2002 by Dee Brestin and Kathy Troccoli

Published by W Publishing Group, a division of Thomas Nelson, Inc.,
P.O. Box 141000, Nashville, Tennessee 37214.

All rights reserved. No portion of this book may be reproduced, stored in a
retrieval system, or transmitted in any form or by any means—electronic, mechanical,
photocopy, recording, or any other—except for brief quotations in printed reviews,
without the prior permission of the publisher.

Unless otherwise noted, Scripture quotations are from the Holy Bible,
New International Version. Copyright © 1973, 1978, 1984, International Bible Society.
Used by permission of Zondervan Bible Publishers.

Scripture quotations noted KJV are from The King James Version of the Bible.

Scripture quotations noted TLB are from The Living Bible, copyright © 1971
by Tyndale House Publishers, Wheaton, Ill. Used by permission.

Scripture quotations noted NKJV are from The New King James Version,
copyright © 1979, 1980, 1982, Thomas Nelson, Inc., Publishers.

Scripture quotations noted PHILLIPS are from J.B. Phillips: The New Testament
in Modern English, Revised Edition. Copyright © J.B. Phillips 1958, 1960, 1972.
Used by permission of Macmillian Publishing Co., Inc.

Library of Congress Cataloging-in-Publication Data

Brestin, Dee, 1944–
    The colors of His love / by Dee Brestin and Kathy Troccoli.
      p. cm.
    Includes bibliographical references.
    ISBN 0-8499-1728-X
    1. Love—Religious aspects—Christianity. I. Troccoli, Kathy. II. Title.
BV4639 .B78 2002
241'.4—dc21   2002013586

Printed in the United States of America
02 03 04 05 BVG 5 4 3 2 1

From Dee:

To my youngest daughter, Annie

> What a transformation has taken place in you—from a five-year-old orphan filled with fear to a beautiful young woman filled with faith, loving others with the mercy of the Father. I see in you, my darling, the colors of His love.

From Dee and Kathy:

To all women who are being transformed into glorious brides

> Listen, O daughter, consider and give ear. . . .
> The king is enthralled by your beauty;
>> honor him, for he is your lord. . . .
>
> All glorious is the princess within her chamber;
>> her gown is interwoven with gold.
> In embroidered garments she is led to the king. (Psalm 45:10–14)

CONTENTS

ACKNOWLEDGMENTS

We (Dee and Kathy) would like to especially thank individuals from W Publishing Group. Mark Sweeney, at the helm, is a man of integrity and vision. Mark, you are also a very wise man to keep Debbie Wickwire on staff, even when it meant flying her regularly from Dallas to Nashville. And Debbie, thank you for getting on all those early morning flights in order to stay with W. We believe your excellence and sensitivity are one of the main reasons authors love W. Ami McConnell, we have learned the wisdom of what Paul said when he warned that we should not despise youth, for you have been a woman of wisdom and skill. We are so thankful you put us together with such a talented editor, Wendy Wood Vahey. Wendy, though we thought it would be an adventure, none of us knew just how great an adventure it would be in your personal life! Tom Williams, thanks for coming up with yet another incredible cover.

We must thank Matt, our amazing manager, who has often pulled off what others have said is impossible. Our assistants, Mary Jo, Nanette, Judy, Beth, and Linda have been terrific in hunting down artwork, meticulously checking footnotes, and keeping us from dropping crucial balls.

And how can we thank our prayer teams, friends, and families enough for interceding so faithfully for us? We are so blessed by your love and faithfulness.

A huge thanks to photographer Bart Larson for allowing us to use his photograph of autumn leaves on pages 102–3. Please check Bart's Web site at www.reflectionsofglory.com.

Overview:
The Secrets of
Transformation

The life of a man who professes to be living
in God must bear the stamp of Christ.

(1 John 2:6 Phillips)

Love one another as I have loved you.

(JOHN 15:12 NKJV)

CHAPTER 1

THE IMPRINT OF A CHRISTIAN

We had just finished a wonderful conference for women. After autographing books at our table, we decided to go out for a relaxing dinner. As Kathy was cutting her burnt steak (that's how she orders it) she glanced at me sideways, smiling:

"You got a little weird with that lady."

"I did not!"

We laughed, as my immediate denial revealed I knew which woman she meant. I changed tactics from denial to defense.

"I thought I was nice . . . Wasn't I nice?"

"No, you weren't. It was a fake nice. You got that funny kind of *I'm a caring Christian woman speaker* plastic smile on your face."

I hit her with my napkin. "I did *not!*"

"You did too, Dee. You had that glazed-over look in your eyes as that poor lady was just trying to get a little attention. Some people just need to talk."

"Well, but . . ."

"Dee, you closed down. You *know* you did."

"Kath. There were a zillion people behind her . . ."

"I know, Dee, but she just needed to share her heart a little."

I paused, finally acknowledging the painful truth. "I hear you . . . I really do."

LET'S GET REAL

When we're really honest with ourselves we have to admit that there are often times when we fail to love, when we fail to care about those around us:

the weary waitress

the coworker grieving the loss of a marriage

the believer who has failed dramatically

the "trying" relative that you see every Christmas

Often our lives lack the passion and vibrancy of a life surrendered to God. We want to be women who love well, but our cups do not overflow with God's love. We want to walk in the light, but we find ourselves moving into the shadows. Like Tinkerbell in *Peter Pan,* when she was losing her power, our lights are dim and our colors are faded. We become dull, like an empty midnight sky. We are no longer stars that glitter in a dark universe. We lack beauty, luster, and life.

As in the story Jesus told of the Good Samaritan, we step over the needy or wounded, preoccupied with our own agenda. Likewise, it is in our very nature to size people up by the way they look, by the way they dress, by the way they talk, and even by how much money they have.

We are easily offended. And when we are genuinely wronged, we often have trouble letting it go. Unwilling to forgive, unwilling to let our wounds heal, we peer over a wall of offenses compiled, holding our weapons of anger and self-righteousness.

We love those who are easy to love, and we like it even more when they love us back. But Jesus asked,

What credit is that to you? Even tax-collectors do that! And if you exchange greetings only with your own circle, are you doing anything exceptional? Even the pagans do that much. (Matthew 5:46–47 PHILLIPS)

We are preoccupied with thoughts about how we look, what others are thinking about us, what we're planning to eat, or watch, or do . . . It's all about us.

Let's face it. The old hymn writers dared to call us "wretches" or even "worms"—and though those terms may be politically incorrect, when we get real, we have to confess that they hit the mark. In the midst of a philosophical discussion a young woman reminded Winston Churchill: "We are all worms."

He responded: "Perhaps, Violet—but I am a glowworm." [1]

Don't you want to be beautiful with the vibrant colors of Jesus? Who wants to stay conformed to the world around him, burrowing through the dirt? There are so many believers who are dead and bitter. They're steeped more in religiosity than in an intimate relationship with Jesus, and they portray that to others. Instead of being alive with the colors of His love, they're watered down to a pasty beige or a murky gray.

Some of you, especially those of you who are quite literal, are thinking: *Now just what* are *the colors of His love?* You would like us to give you a list, like the colors of the rainbow, and tell you what each represents. We can't do that any more than we can list all the glorious colors God created in the feathers of the peacock, the petals of the wildflowers, or the leaves of the autumn. God is so varied in the ways He blesses, so lavish in the ways He bestows His love upon us. We can't possibly put a boundary around the infinite creativity of God. However, we are going to show you through the powerful Word of God the secrets to becoming transformed into a vibrant woman of God who clearly displays His lovely colors and, therefore, the distinguishing imprint of a Christian.

(Dee) Recently, I showed my grandchildren how to make an imprint of a leaf. I gave them each a crayon in an autumn color and a leaf from a backyard tree. Seven-year-old Emily, the eldest, led the way. She placed an oak

leaf under a piece of white paper and rubbed the long side of an unwrapped Indian red crayon over the top. The more she rubbed, the more an elongated oak leaf emerged. She grinned, showing the space where her two front teeth had been, and held up her creation proudly for her siblings to admire.

Five-year-old Jessa was in earnest as she rubbed a harvest gold crayon over an elm leaf. "Gramma, look!" She gave a little cry of delight as the imprint appeared: the stem, the veins, the tiny teeth all around the edge—a distinct and perfectly compact elm leaf.

Three-year-old Simeon hopped up on the chair, insisting: "I can do it!" With a little help and encouragement to be gentle, he rubbed a blazing crimson crayon over a maple leaf. He beamed as it emerged. "I did it! I did it!" And he had. There it was—that most familiar of leaves, the maple, aflame in autumn loveliness.

There was no mistaking an oak for an elm, or an elm for a maple. Each had its own distinct imprint.

What *is* the imprint of a Christian?

THE GREATEST OF THESE IS LOVE

Jim is a friend who works with troubled youth. Through the help of God he's found freedom from drugs and other prisons. Because Jim has a rough manner and poor grammar, people might easily dismiss him, but he is a true man of God, bearing the distinct imprint of a Christian. He stopped by just this morning. With his usual carefree attitude, he plopped himself on the couch. He noticed I was in the middle of writing and asked how he could pray for me. When I told him that Kathy and I had been working on a book about loving others the way Jesus does, he grinned, saying,

> "Yeah, that's the real deal. When kids at the center ask me what Christians do, I go, 'They love on people.'"
>
> I smiled, loving Jim's concise description and wishing it were always true.
>
> Jim continued, "And then they ask me, 'Even the ones that make you wanna puke?'"

Thoughts raced through my head, thinking of a few of the "hard-to-love"
people in my life.

Jim's face was filled with compassion as he reflected. "Dee, you can't imag-
ine the junk thrown at these kids—at home they get cussed at, beat, and worse
. . . And so I tell them: 'Especially them. It's no big deal to love the easy ones.
Love starts with the hard ones. That's where Jesus comes in.'"

Kathy, like my friend Jim, is real. One of the many reasons Kathy is loved
the way she is comes from her authenticity. The Lord has given her an ability to cut right to the heart of the matter. Even as a baby Christian, she came
to the Scriptures with the kind of childlike faith and simplicity that Jesus
tells us we all need. The following story she tells illustrates this so clearly, but
we want to preface it by saying that this is not to be interpreted as bashing a
particular belief, for that is the exact opposite of the message of this book.
The Lord has given us a deep love and appreciation for the church, the body
of true believers, and for the unique dimensions that various denominations
can bring to the body of Christ. But this story illustrates how sometimes
even believers can fail to leave the stamp of Christ. We confuse the genuine
imprint with a lot of other things, influenced by what our particular denomination or circle of friends emphasizes as important.

(Kathy) I was a new Christian when I was getting asked to sing at many
different places on Long Island and in New York City. I was immediately
thrown into a sea of churches: Assembly of God, Catholic, Baptist . . . I
was often drowning in the confusion of all the different theologies I was
hearing.

Speak in tongues.
Don't speak in tongues.
Be immersed.
Be sprinkled.
Raise your hands.
Don't raise your hands.
Sing quietly.

Sing loudly.
Don't sing at all.

I'd often come home from singing at church events or coffeehouses with a heavy heart. I found that the simple realization that Jesus loved me and wanted me to love others was suddenly clouded by what seemed like so many divisive ways of expressing Christianity. Arrogance permeated so many places. People thought their church "did it right." People thought their beliefs were "the true beliefs." People thought everyone else was "a little off base." It affected me deeply because in my naiveté, I expected we would live together as one big happy family, being cherished by a big and holy God. I remember being saddened at the creeping feelings of disillusionment that were slowly smothering my newfound joy.

I came home late one night, after singing at yet another church service. I went into my bedroom and sat on the floor against the wall. I was weary, confused, and discouraged. Looking up to God I said,

Lord, I don't know what to make of all of this.
If this is Christianity —I'm not sure I want it.

I let out a big sigh and remained quiet for a while. My kite had been soaring so high and now it felt as if it were taking a nosedive. Since then I've learned it is in times like these, in the stillness, that Jesus comes gently. This is what I sensed He was saying to me that night:

Open the Gospels. Look at Me. Look at My life.
Take in the things I've said. I will teach you.

He is so wonderful like that. When we are at the end of *ourselves*, He comes to us and shows us *Himself.* Even now when moments of frustration arise, when there is obvious hypocrisy or twisting of the Word of God, I go back to that moment.

I continued to travel all over the New York area and had quickly become a national recording artist. At the time, I traveled by myself, with just my guitar and a little box of records to sell. I was constantly meeting new people: in hotels, on planes, at lunches and dinners. Conversations with complete strangers had become a way of life.

One particular time, I was invited to eat lunch at a restaurant with a senior pastor and some people from his congregation. We sat at a very long table because there were twelve of us. I was on one end and the pastor was on the other. We were all immersed in little clusters of conversation. All of a sudden the pastor said,

"Kathy, can I ask you something?"
All conversations ceased. All eyes turned to me.
"Sure, Pastor."

Because this was the first time he had spoken directly to me, I was expecting the simple exchanges of getting to know one another, such as: *Where are you from? How was your flight?* Or even, *How was your lunch?* Instead, this is what he asked me:

"Are you baptized in the Holy Spirit?"

An awkward silence engulfed the table. Many thoughts raced through my mind. *Am I before a jury here? Is everyone waiting for the* right *answer? Why would he ask me this? If I say, "Yes," am I in the club? If I say, "No," are they all going to lay hands on me right here at the table?*

I don't want to address the subject of baptism by the Holy Spirit here. What I *do* want to address is how we approach one another. Do we have sensitivity, gracious timing, and respect for another's beliefs? We are often more concerned with people's "spiritual state" than with trying to understand or get to know them. We don't know their background, their religion, their culture—we may not even know their names—yet we quickly present our agenda.

At that moment, I didn't feel like the pastor cared about *me.* In fact, I felt somewhat shamed. The only thought that came to my head and quickly out of my mouth was:

"Well, Pastor, are you asking me if I love well?"

He responded with a nervous laugh. I just smiled and went on in conversation, asking about him and his family. I knew my words to the pastor seemed pointed but they simply were an overflow of what I had been reading in the Gospels and my recent frustration of how we express our Christianity. My sister had recently married, and at the service I read 1 Corinthians 13.

> *If I speak in the tongues of men and of angels, but have not love, I am only a resounding gong or a clanging cymbal . . .*
> *If I give all I possess to the poor and surrender my body to the flames, but have not love, I gain nothing.* (1 Corinthians 13:1, 3)

The Bible is so clear that if we don't have love, we have nothing. I guess I wanted this man to be inquisitive about me, or I wanted at least to sense that he cared about *me*. As believers, we may be quick to give our thoughts on salvation, or doctrine, or even immorality, and what we say may be true and vital, but if we don't care about an individual's state of mind or heart, the person will certainly know it. You would be surprised how much more respect you get from someone when you really listen and show him you care.

Isn't it wonderful that God is a perfect gentleman? He is chivalrous and sensitive. He is love. And if we are going to bear His imprint, then we *must* be His love.

So often we make the mark of a Christian something quite different from what Jesus commanded and lived out. For example,

A priest might have asked:
"Are you going to confession and communion regularly?"

A Methodist or Episcopalian might have questioned:
"Are you volunteering in our soup kitchen?"

A Baptist might have wondered:
"Are you having your daily quiet time?"

(Have we officially offended everyone by now?) All of those things may be good things, but it is possible to be doing them all and yet *not* bear the imprint of Christ. When people brush up against us, the way Dee's grandchildren brushed their crayons across their leaves, what is the imprint that comes forth?

Jesus tells us what it must be. The imprint is His distinctive love. This is how we leave, as J. B. Phillips puts it, "the stamp of Christ." This is the identifiable image of Christ that should come forth when someone interacts with you, whether it is a quick brush or a more intense interaction.

THE MOST IMPORTANT THING

(Dee) Often we say the most heartfelt things when time is running out. When I wrote *The Friendships of Women* many years ago, I wrote a paragraph that turned out to be prophetic:

> *If God permits me the knowledge, I will sit at the bedside of a dying parent or friend. Though the sorrow may be deep, I will not consider it wasted sadness. My presence may give the one I love comfort. Closing expressions of love may give consolation for years to come. The more final the good-bye, the greater the sadness, but the more cherished the memory.*[2]

This year, on my way to a speaking engagement in Dallas, I received a call that my dad had suffered a massive stroke. I flew to California to be at his side in the intensive care ward. For eight days I sat with him, wondering if he knew I was there. His eyes were closed, his breathing, labored. Those eight days were some of the hardest and yet the most precious of my life. Dad had always been a giant in my eyes: a man of integrity, a man of intellect, a man of strong opinions (not all of which I shared), but a man absolutely committed to his wife and three daughters. Now life was ebbing from him. He seemed so frail, so helpless. My mother, his bride of sixty-five years, sang him love songs, breaking my heart with:

"Let me call you Sweetheart, I'm in love with you . . ."

She was telling him the most important thing. She was telling him of her love for him.

My sisters and I did the same.

One night, after a long day at the hospital, I went back to my parents' home. As I sat at Dad's desk, I was comforted to spy a gift I'd given to him one Father's Day. It was a clothbound journal, in which I had written a reason, on each page, why I loved him. Though it was several years old, there it was, right on his desk. I slipped it in my purse to read to him at the hospital. I didn't know when he would die, though it seemed likely it would be soon. I kept changing my return flight home. Finally, God gave me a peace about saying good-bye. With tears I pleaded with the Lord to give me a special moment with him, one in which Dad would open his eyes and hear me, *really hear me*.

When I walked into his room, I was overwhelmed because, for the first time, his eyes were open. When someone is prayed for so diligently, you know God is faithful to bring His abiding presence—especially at the end of his life. This is exactly what I sensed at my father's bedside. With tears streaming down my cheeks, I held his weakened hands, telling him the most important things—of my love, and of God's love for him. He was watching me intently. My adult son John sat by watching, weeping, and praying.

"Mom," he said, "look at how his eyes are fixed on yours. He's hearing you."

I shared about Jesus once again, and then I read to him from the journal, telling him the reasons I loved him. I thanked him for his devotion to Mother, for his enthusiasm for life, for introducing me to the classics, for taking me to faraway places, for loving dogs, for *always* being there when I needed him. One of the pages I read was:

> *Thank you, Dad, for always being at the gate whenever I came home. I knew I could count on you. As soon as I walked out of the plane, I'd see your eyes intent on the door, watching for me. Then your handsome face would light up and you'd cry: "There she is!" Then you'd laugh and open your arms for our great hug.*

I began to sob.

"Please Daddy, *please, please.* Be at the gate."

Those were the last words I spoke to him. He died two days later.

What do we say when time is running out? The most important things.

Kathy and I were scheduled to begin writing this book on Tuesday, September 11, 2001, at 9 A.M. We had gone to my cabin in Door County, Wisconsin, for time away from the world, where we could really concentrate. I was all set up and ready to go: I had our working table facing the waves of Green Bay, the coffee was brewing, and the fire was crackling in the fireplace. For four days we would write. I was putting on my jacket to go get Kathy at her hotel, when the phone rang.

(Kathy) I had turned on the television as I was getting ready to take a shower. There it was: an airplane flying into one of the World Trade Towers. I was horrified. I began to weep. I called Dee to tell her to turn on her TV. We quickly hung up. The other plane hit the second tower. I sat on my bed completely paralyzed. My beloved city was crumbling right before my eyes. A knock at the door awakened me from the nightmare that I wished *were* just a dream. It was Dee. I fell into her arms and we both sobbed. All we could do was cry out to Jesus. We continued to watch the news together. As the day wore on, we learned what had actually happened: an evil had descended on this nation, taking with it thousands of lives. Story upon story unfolded of people calling from hijacked planes and burning buildings.

Men calling wives to say, "I love you."
Sons calling mothers to say, "I love you."
Sisters calling brothers to say, "I love you."

What do we say at the end? The most important thing.

TELL THEM I LOVE THEM

It's remarkable that as Jesus neared the cross, He wanted to convey the same message as those who were about to die on that tragic September day: "Let them know that I love them."

First He told them,

My children, I will be with you only a little longer. (John 13:33a)

Then He reminded them of His love and gave them a command:

As I have loved you, so you must love one another. (John 13:34b)

Do you see? He loves us. And we are not only to *tell* others of His love, we are to *be* His love, *give* His love, *live* His love. We are to bear this imprint to one another. Jesus was very clear about this. He went on to say:

By this all men will know that you are my disciples, if you love one another. (John 13:35)

When you brush a crayon across a leaf, you can see its veins, its stem, its unique shape. The identity of the tree that birthed that leaf, that gave it life, is distinctive.

What is the imprint of a believer? Is it obvious who gave us birth? Can they see His hands, His eyes, His heart, His love? When people brush up against us, are they intrigued and inquisitive about the source of our love? Do they recognize Jesus?

It is no coincidence that the message gets muddied and the imprint faded.

It is no coincidence that the message gets distorted and the imprint counterfeited.

If the church were a heart, its current failure to love is like a massive heart attack. We, as the arteries, get clogged with judgment, hate, pride, and gossip. How can His lifeblood flow through us toward each other, let alone into a world so desperate for the love of Christ?

THE MARK OF A CHRISTIAN

(Dee) I went through some of the same struggles Kathy did when I began my journey into Christianity. So many messages came at me, and I was trying to

discern who was "right" and what was most important. God ministered to me through an eloquent little book entitled *The Mark of a Christian* by Francis Schaeffer, a man who was a prophet in his time, cutting to the core, discerning where the church was headed. Dr. Schaeffer stressed that not only did Jesus *command* us to be His love, He *prayed* we would be His love in John 17. This passage has been called His "High Priestly Prayer." *When* did Jesus pray this? Near the end of His life on earth, when time was running out, just before He was betrayed. We must listen carefully. In this prayer He again tells us the mark of a Christian.

For three years, Jesus has lived under a death sentence, which is now just days away. Jesus prayed first for His disciples, but then He looked down through the generations, to you and to me, and said:

> *My prayer is not for them alone. I pray also for those who will believe in me through their message . . .* (John 17:20)

And what did He pray for us?

> *. . . that all of them may be one, Father, just as you are in me and I am in you. May they also be in us so that the world may believe that you have sent me.* (John 17:21)

Do you see? Unless we genuinely love each other, unless we truly care for each other, unless we are living in harmony, *the world will not believe.* There is so much dissension out there: quarreling, misunderstanding, and belittling. The world lives like this. The world lives without hope. We do much of the same. Why would anybody *without* Jesus want our life *with* Jesus if it looks the same? Believe me, they're watching. *We* watch! Why wouldn't they be watching?

Everybody wants the real deal. And when you show the real deal, the purity of love, it is hard to resist. There is no moving toward God without love. If we who bear His name do not love, Jesus tells us the world will dismiss *Him.* This is sobering, because we all know Christians who do not bear this imprint, and each of us at one time or another could step to the front of that line. Jesus gives us *two* commands about loving others: we are to love our neighbor as ourselves; we are to love our *brother* as Christ loved us. Both love commands are vital and both kinds of love are to be seen in the mark of a Christian. It certainly would be ugly to love *just* other believers and not our neighbor. Yet Scripture stresses that there is something terribly important about loving our *brother.* When unbelievers witnessed the great love between the believers in the book of Acts, when they saw how they took care of their poor, when they saw how strong the bond was between believers, they were drawn to Jesus as well. Again and again it is repeated in the New Testament that it is absolutely vital that we, in the body of Christ, show love for one another. See these dual commands, including the emphasis on the new command:

> *Therefore, as we have opportunity, let us do good to all people, especially to those who belong to the family of believers.* (Galatians 6:10)

Francis Schaeffer explains:

> *The church is to judge whether a man is a Christian on the basis of his doctrine . . . and then his credible profession of faith . . . But we cannot expect the world to judge that way, because the world cares nothing about doctrine . . .*
>
> *Jesus turns to the world and says, "I've something to say to you. On the basis of my authority, I give you a right: you may judge whether or not an individual is a Christian on the basis of the love he shows to all Christians."*
>
> *We are not to choose between loving all men as ourselves and loving Christians in a special way . . . but we can understand how overwhelmingly important it is that all men be able to see an observable love for those with whom we have these special ties.*
>
> *. . . We must be very careful at this point, however. We may be true Christians, really born-again Christians, and yet fail in love toward other Christians. As a matter of fact, to be completely realistic, it is stronger than this. There will be times (and let us say it with tears), there will be times when we will fail in our love toward each other as Christians.*
>
> *The point is that it is possible to be a Christian without showing the mark, but if we expect non-Christians to know that we are Christians, we must show the mark.*[3]

How can we be certain to show the mark? How can we be transformed?

Christianity 101

This is the exciting part, for John wrote a letter that could be called Christianity 101, giving us basic principles that can transform us into beautiful women of God. If you are a man reading this, the principles will work for you too. The backbone of this book is four principles found in John's first letter. These four transforming principles of Christlike love—for His love is different from the world's love—are based on

Light,
Death,
Truth,
Mercy.

God is so wonderful in that in addition to giving us principles, He gives us pictures of people to help us *really* see His truth. Cain, for example, refused the light of God. His destructive life is a vivid illustration of what will happen to us if we do likewise. Esther, in contrast, is changed into a beautiful woman because she embraced all of these transforming principles. We are also excited, as we tell you these stories, to show you paintings from the Masters—incredible portraits of Cain, Esther, and of others. We will show you these paintings in black and white, and in their lovely colors in the video, if you are doing the accompanying Bible study (to be released Spring 2003).

Just as the gift of music is a way of expressing God's truth and beauty, so is the gift of art. An artist is like a Bible commentator, in that he portrays the account as he sees it. It may be a slightly different perspective from yours, but it is always good to look at Scripture from a fellow traveler's perspective. Slow down, and see what you can discover. Not only can these artists open windows of understanding for us, their portraits can etch the truths in our memories, helping us become what God longs for us to be.

To give you a taste of what is to come, one of the primary principles in John's first letter is that a child of God shows Christlike love to his brother. Actively loving our brother will help us to know we "belong to the truth." John writes:

If anyone has material possessions and sees his brother in need but has no pity
on him, how can the love of God be in him? Dear children, let us not love with
words or tongue but with actions and in truth. This then is how we know that we
belong to the truth . . . (1 John 3:17–19a)

This principle springs to life with a picture, the story that Jesus told of the
Good Samaritan. In the story (Luke 10:30–37), the believers hurried past
the victim (the man who had been beaten and robbed), preoccupied with
their own agendas, but the Samaritan, an unbeliever despised by the Jews,
had compassion and stopped to help.

THE GOOD SAMARITAN

JACOPO BASSANO (1517/18–1592)

Jesus was not saying that the Samaritan was a believer, nor that the priest
or the Levite who hurried past the wounded man were unbelievers, but that
the Samaritan was doing a better job of bearing the mark of a Christian. We

meet people all the time who put some Christians to shame. If they are so impressive as unbelievers, we often wonder what they'd be like if they committed their lives to Christ.

Her eloquence—how would she speak for Jesus?
His faithfulness—how could that be directed for the Lord?
Her compassion—how many lives would be touched by the heart of God?

If an unbeliever who had good things poured into his soul through a healthy family can bear the mark of God, then *we* who know the Lord should be radiant, filled with the colors of His love. Our imprints can become vivid masterpieces if we learn to apply the principles of John's letter.

(*Kathy*) Loving others can seem like such an obvious principle, yet we often fail to do so. I have found that when I actively love someone, it sucks the poison out of my heart. If it is a person that I don't really know, such as the clerk at the grocery store, when I show her love, I find myself caring more, seeing her through God's eyes. If that person is someone who was unkind to me, by actively showing them compassion and forgiveness, I find I have more mercy toward them, and that the irritation or hurt begins to be absorbed. This simple principle of John's letter transforms me.

John has often been called the apostle of love, and the primary purpose of his first letter is to tell us *how* to bear the imprint of a Christian. We are all works in progress, and in some of us the imprint is barely discernible and the colors are pale. John's simple yet profound principles, if obeyed, will make the imprint distinct and the colors vivid. These principles *will* transform you with the radiance of Christ.

When we approached writing our first book together, *Falling in Love with Jesus*, each of us thought: *I love Jesus, but do I live in a constant state of abandonment to Him?* We knew we didn't. Yet we wrote because a deeper love relationship is the cry of our hearts and we *are* seeing progress as we continue to abandon ourselves to God and grow in the grace and knowledge of Jesus Christ.

So here we are again. *We love others, but we also fail miserably.* We are all humbled by the good Samaritans around us. Yet as we fall at the foot of the cross and absorb all of what it represents, a power will be unleashed, transforming us into women who love well. We are promised that.

We pray that we may live lives full of the love of Jesus Christ. We pray that for you as well. May we never grow cold, dull, and gray. May we never become like snow that has lingered too long in a city, collecting soot, sitting in crusty, dirty piles along the sidewalk.

TRANSFORMATION

We both travel a great deal, and very often early flights are involved. Even though that can be exhausting, the one good thing is that they allow us to see the sunrise from the air. Have you ever experienced this? It is a breathtaking way to start the day. Looking out our windows before takeoff, the sky is normally blue-black. The city is sleeping. As we soar above the clouds, the light of the majestic orange-yellow sun transforms *everything*. What a beautiful sight. As the minutes pass by we are certain that this same light will stream into kitchen windows, set farmlands ablaze, and glisten like diamonds on city skyscrapers. Tiny churches and grand cathedrals will become iridescent because of the penetrating light through their stained-glass windows.

The sun definitely touches the world with a unique beauty. The light of Jesus Christ can do the same through us. We can touch the world with the colors of His love.

Whoever does not love does not know God, because God is love.

(1 John 4:8)

Chapter 2

Black and White

(Kathy)

I have shared in concert and expressed in my books my love for the Baker boys: Logan, Jordan, and Jared. They are six, four, and two, and a delight to my soul. They are comical, playful, and awfully rambunctious. In my recent stay at their home in Anderson, Indiana, I smothered them with hugs and kisses and got plenty in return. The guest bedroom is right off of the kitchen, so, needless to say, I don't need an alarm clock. One morning Jared, the two-year-old, burst through my door and hopped on my bed.

"Coli, Coli, wake up!"

As he bounced up and down on the mattress, I groggily reached for him and drew him close. He squirmed his way out, but I got enough of a morning hug to start my day.

"Get up, Coli! I want to show you my Spider-Man play."

I thought, *Spider-Man? This should be interesting.* As always, I was drawn by his sweetness. I dragged myself out of bed, grinning in anticipation. He raced down the hall with just a T-shirt on and no bottoms, delighted that I

21

was following him. When we entered his bedroom it was completely dark except for a little flashlight he had rigged up to the bedpost. It was shining on two chairs that he put side by side for the audience (his mom and me).

Allyson and I sat down with exaggerated excitement. He then stood right in front of us and spoke with all the theatrics of a magician. He whispered intensely:

"Get ready . . . to be amazed."

Allyson and I looked at each other and wanted to burst out laughing.

WHAT AN AWAKENING!

When I left the Bakers' house I reminisced, as I always do. It's always a precious time for me with those boys. Jared's statement kept playing over and over again in my head. With all the responsibilities that come upon me each day, I could easily become anxious and discouraged. But when I rest in God, placing my trust once again in Him and His promises, I hear Jared's words ring out to me, as if from the mouth of God:

Get ready to be amazed.

Can you remember when you first discovered who Jesus was? What an awakening! Your heart and mind were opened to a whole new world. You started thinking way beyond earthly things. For some of us, it was almost a euphoric state. Each new day held a different promise. We finally understood the reason for the deep ache in our souls. We finally understood our loneliness—it was for our Maker. Answers to some of our questions were revealed.

For many of us, however, a time comes when the reality of life sets in again. We wake from our honeymoon, open the curtains, and observe the true state of affairs:

Life is still hard.
We still get lonely.
People are still ugly.

There is still pain.
There are still injustices.
Evil still pervades our world.

It can all seem so discouraging. Our initial passion wanes. We begin to lose the enthusiasm and strength we once held in our hearts to take the high and narrow road.

We knew God would lead us when He asked us to follow Him, but we didn't know we would follow Him through some dark places. Our immaturity led us to believe that the hard would get less hard, and the easy would get easier.

So subtly and slowly, we find ourselves questioning all the things we so earnestly embraced in the beginning. We find ourselves asking:

Now, why *do I want to be holy?*

The cost is great. Our flesh wages war against everything God stands for. We just don't know if we have it in us. We want to be His, but do we want to be holy? Instead of pushing on with the passion that once drove us toward the high places, we become complacent and settle into a comfortable nest of mediocrity. We no longer dream of flying. We'd rather stay put. We think:

I don't want to work that hard.
I don't want to be that challenged.
I don't want to be that honest.

All we can see is the cost. The wonder is gone. We are no longer prepared, each day, to be amazed.

God knows us. He made us. He knows we have unfaithful hearts and that we will lose the excitement of our first love. So, thousands of years ago, He appointed John to write to you and to me. How can we retain our enthusiasm? How can we possibly love the way He wants us to love? There are unexpected secrets in this letter that will empower us to become women who love well, to become radiant women.

HE HAS LAVISHED LOVE UPON YOU

We cherish the opportunity that God has given us to share His life with you and to pray over you. Every day many of us deal with anxieties and fears that make us "lose our way" and doubt His love for us. It is wonderful to see women light up when we speak God's very own words over them.

You are the object of His affection.
He has you engraved on the palms of His hands.
You are His Beloved.
How great is the love the Father has lavished upon you!

What a privilege to be sharing with you, from Scripture, the glorious promises and portraits of His love. We see the longing, the hunger in your eyes, for within each of us, dark voices whisper, taunting:

You don't deserve to be loved.
No one could know your darkest secrets and still love you.
You're such a fraud.
You keep blowing it. What's the point?

Where do you think these thoughts come from?

ANCIENT OF FOES

He is called "the father of lies." He is known as "the accuser of the brethren." He is our enemy, Satan himself. Jesus wants us to walk on His bridge of truth to get us to the high places. But, like termites, deception and doubt have burrowed themselves into our bridge. We are now vulnerable to the elements, the unexpected storms of life. The enemy knows these are coming, so he erodes our confidence in the Lord, causing our bridge of truth to tremble. He wants us to doubt God's mercies. He wants us to doubt God's love. He plainly just wants us to doubt God. Soon we find ourselves thinking:

Does He really know what is best for me?
Can I really trust Him?

Surely He knows I'm not going to be able to live out a life of holiness.
It seems like an awful lot of hard work for little return.

We hesitate. We wonder if it will be worth it.

As women we often let our hearts lead us. But our sensitivity can also be used against us, and the enemy has done that time and time again. One of his favorite strategies is to attack our confidence in God by playing on our emotions and fears. As our doubts grow, our ability to resist temptation weakens. Soon we may begin to wonder if we really know Him, if we are really capable of living the Christian life, or if we can, indeed, overcome all that is in the world.

That's why the first letter of John is vital for us to study, for John tells us that if we put into practice the principles he shares, holiness *will* take root in us. He then gives us secrets for "how we set our hearts at rest in his presence whenever our hearts condemn us" (1 John 3:19b–20a). Those secrets are surprising. *Get ready to be amazed.*

YOU'RE SO BLACK AND WHITE

On first reading, John's letter may seem quite confusing. Instead of increasing our confidence, it can make us feel woefully inadequate. He seems to say that if you are a *true* child of God you will:

always stay in the light
always obey
always love your brother
always embrace the truth

John speaks in polarities, in blacks and whites. This can seem impossible to live out. It's easy to feel overwhelmed. Consider:

Whoever hates his brother is in the darkness . . . (1 John 2:11a)

If anyone loves the world, the love of the Father is not in him. (1 John 2:15b)

No one who lives in him keeps on sinning. (1 John 3:6a)

He who does what is sinful is of the devil . . . (1 John 3:8a)

Whoever does not love does not know God, because God is love. (1 John 4:8)

Do you see what we mean? Each of us knows we have failed at every single one of the above. So we wonder:

Is he kidding?
I wander in the darkness a lot. Am I damned?
Am I "of the devil" because I sin every day?

It could make you run for the hills.

However, these "black and white" statements must be read in the context of the whole letter. John makes it clear that even though we are believers, we *will* fail. For example, he says:

> *If we claim to be without sin, we deceive ourselves and the truth is not in us.* (1 John 1:8)

> *My dear children, I write this to you so that you will not sin. But if anybody does sin, we have one who speaks to the Father in our defense—Jesus Christ, the Righteous One.* (1 John 2:1)

So, which is it? Does a child of God sin or not? What *is* John saying?

A CHILD BEARS THE IMPRINT OF HIS PARENT

Kathy has many of the wonderful characteristics of her mother, Josephine. Her mother was smart and organized. She was a great administrator and delegated well. I see this clearly in Kathy. Even while we are working, she is continually adding things to her "to do" list. She keeps a dozen balls in the air, like so many fragile ornaments, with very few crashing and breaking. She is like her mother in this.

Kathy has also admitted to sharing some negative characteristics of her mother. Josephine liked things "just so." Kathy has shared with me that her mother liked the towels folded a certain way before they were put in the closet. She wanted the carrots cut a certain way before they were put in the salad. She wanted the Christmas ornaments placed exactly in the right boxes before they were put back in the attic. It drove Kathy crazy. Now she admits she drives those close to her a little crazy with the same compulsive tendencies.

Since I have grown close to Kathy I see that, like Josephine, she is a perfectionist. Even in the midst of intense writing days, it is not unusual for her to pick a piece of lint from my sweater, push my bangs back, or mention an ink smudge on my finger. She notices everything. Her office is beautiful, classy, and immaculate. Every drawer is in order. Every closet is perfectly organized. Even her attic is dust free. Sometimes I'll catch her getting way too particular about some small detail, and I'll say, "Okay, Josephine."

She'll immediately take the hint and say, "I know, I know. I'm sorry."

Kathy often talks and sings about her mom. A song she wrote called "Good-Bye for Now," has encouraged thousands of people as they feel the loss of their loved ones. One night as she had just finished singing this poignant ballad, she tossed a kiss up to heaven. Women were literally passing boxes of Kleenex down the rows, wiping their tears.

Then Kathy continued to share, "I don't think there will ever be a time when I don't miss my mother. In fact, the other day, I was in a store and bought this little gadget. It is called 'a portable parent.' I had to buy it because it reminded me so much of my dear, sweet, precious mother."

People began to simmer down and waited with sensitive anticipation. Kathy placed the gadget close to the microphone and flipped the switch. This is what the audience heard:

"Have you got on clean underwear? You might be in an accident."

The audience was stunned for a moment, then broke into a thunderous guffaw. Kathy pressed another button that allowed the room to hear this battery-operated "mother." The irritatingly metallic voice said:

"It will never get better if you pick at it."

Then she pressed the third button.

"It's broken. Are you happy now?"

The audience went completely wild. It was welcome comic relief.

We tend to reflect the image of our parents, the good and the bad. Ezekiel 16:44 quotes the familiar proverb: "Like mother, like daughter." A child tends to reflect, genetically, the physical and often the personality traits of his parents. This is true in a spiritual sense as well. If the consistent direction of your life is to walk in the darkness and to hate your brother, you should, indeed, be concerned if you are really a child of God. If the consistent life direction of someone who claims to be a Christian does not reflect the life of God, he or she may be a counterfeit, and John warns us to be alert to the counterfeit "believers" among us so we are not led astray. There *are* wolves in sheep's clothing who may lead us astray with false teaching, may marry and exploit our daughters, and may devour us. We must look for fruit, and if it is not there, we must be alert to the counterfeit. We must recognize when someone is not the real thing, and we should be more concerned with *our* being the real thing.

That doesn't mean we will never fail. We are human. But it does mean, as children of God, because He is perfection, because He is love, and because He is holy, that we should reflect the One who gave us spiritual birth. J. B. Phillips' paraphrase captures what John is saying:

> The man who lives a consistently good life is a good man, as surely as God is good. But the man whose life is habitually sinful is spiritually a son of the devil, for the devil is behind all sin, as he always has been. Now the Son of God came to earth with the express purpose of liquidating the devil's activities. The man who is really God's son does not practice sin, for God's nature is in him, for good, and such a heredity is incapable of sin. (1 John 3:8–9 PHILLIPS)

(Dee) When our firstborn, J. R., was about three, he used to ask people: "Do you love Jesus or the devil?" It would obviously embarrass Steve and me, and put our guests on the spot, but you know what? I am beginning to understand how profound his question actually was. John's letter makes it clear that either our parent is the Father of Light or the father of darkness.

As we mature, we become more and more like the one who gave us birth. This truth permeates John's letter.

John therefore says that *God's* child does not make a practice of sin. That is such a powerful statement. He knows we *will* sin. He understands our capabilities. But His desire is that we do not have a "life direction" of it.

That is what Jesus meant when He said to the adulteress, "Go and sin no more." *Don't let it be your life choice.* That's how we begin to reflect His image. What is the imprint of a Christian? It is the imprint of the Lord. As we begin to understand John's black-and-white statements, we see the power in them to transform us into reflections of the Lord. Do you see?

> Because God is light
> > we *must* stay in the light.
> Because Jesus laid down His life
> > we *must* die to ourselves.
> Because God is truth,
> > we *must* live by the truth.
> Because God is mercy,
> > we *must* be merciful.

Here is the exciting part. We *will* have victory over our condemning hearts, over the lies of the enemy, and over a faded and colorless life, *if* we:

> stay in the light,
> die to ourselves,
> walk by the truth,
> and live lives of mercy.

(Kathy) Now by this point, you must be reading this saying, *Okay, Kathy and Dee, that's just what I'll do. Yeah, right.* It's like when I was thirty pounds overweight, my thin sister said, "Well, Kath, just eat less." We understand how all of this sounds so great and godly. As a matter of fact, it can seem unattainable because of our human frailty. But remember: the Spirit that raised Jesus from the dead lives in us. We *can* do all things. He will supply what He demands.

The more you walk in the light, the stronger the light of Christ will become in you.

The more you die to yourself, the more Christ will live in you.

The more you live by truth, the more you will be set free to be like Christ.

The more you love your brother, the more you will show the mercy of Christ.

Choosing a life direction of the above things:

The stronger the imprint of Jesus will be in you.

Get ready to be amazed.

For the wedding of the Lamb has come, and his bride has made herself ready.
Fine linen, bright and clean, was given her to wear.

(REVELATION 19:7B–8A)

CHAPTER 3

EMBROIDERED WITH GOLD

Falling in Love with Jesus was the theme of a two-day event for women in ministry. It was being held at an elegant hotel in Atlanta. Approximately four hundred women were going to attend.

(Dee) My plane arrived first. I waited with Mary Frances, the retreat coordinator, outside of the security area. Darlene, a Delta flight attendant who could easily get through security, went to meet Kathy at her gate. Kathy's plane came in, but Darlene called Mary Frances on her cell phone with panic in her voice:

"Kathy wasn't on the plane."

"Did you ask them to check the passenger list?"

"I did, and she's listed. But I watched every passenger get off, and she wasn't on the plane."

"Mary Frances," I said, "Kathy was on the plane. Trust me. Darlene just didn't recognize her. People always look for the 'album cover Kathy.' You know—the hair done, the makeup, the gorgeous clothes. Don't worry. I'll watch for her. She'll be coming up the escalator any minute."

Sure enough, a few minutes later, there she was, easily lost in the crowd in her typical ball cap, jeans, cowboy boots, and leather jacket. I waved my arms to get her attention. She smiled that recognizable smile, and they all breathed a sigh of relief.

A SURPRISING BRIDE

It turned out to be the most amazing weekend. It was a unique experience for both of us. In our book *Falling in Love with Jesus* we described the beautiful romance in the relationship of the bride and the bridegroom as it pertains to our relationship with Jesus, but at this event we had never expected to experience all the pomp and circumstance that's involved with a royal wedding reception. We watched as women in ministry completely absorbed the pampering, the attention, and the reminder that they are loved as the Bride of Christ. We'd love to take you through some of the happenings of those couple of days. Our desire is for every woman to experience the joy and beauty that the weekend held.

Facials, manicures, and massages were available, without cost, before the start of the event. There were white flowers and displays of wedding gowns throughout the hotel. When you walked into the ballroom, each table was set up with a different elaborate centerpiece: one had an antique candelabra, fully lit, another had a vase of a dozen white roses, and another had gifts in gold wrapping draped with strings of pearls. Candles glowed everywhere, causing the fine china and crystal on every table to gleam. The stage was set up with garlands of roses draped between white columns. In the evening, when the women returned to their rooms, they found rose petals and chocolates scattered across their bedspreads. The dessert was a three-tiered, elegantly decorated wedding cake. It was all magnificent.

Of course we arrived much earlier than the guests to prepare for the weekend. Our van pulled up to a side entrance, which was lined with urns overflowing with flowers.

(Kathy) I was walking in to greet the women when I was stopped.

"Wait, wait, wait! You can't come in yet."

Dee and I began to see what was so sweetly planned. The women started to unroll a white lace runner. A bubble machine was turned on over the door, and bubbles began to fill the air. When I saw what they were doing, I lightheartedly pushed Dee aside, saying:

"You've done this before.
Get out of the way!
This may be my only chance!"

This was a moment I didn't want to rush. I began to walk with an exaggerated "bride step," singing "Here Comes the Bride." Everyone laughed hysterically. Part of the comedy was that instead of wearing a delicate white wedding gown and demure veil, I marched in wearing my traveling clothes: jeans, leather jacket, and ball cap. I had on no makeup, and to be quite honest, I had to catch a really early flight, so I had not even showered. I was surely not a typical bride!

It hit us later that this picture was a quite accurate portrayal of our true state as His betrothed . . .

WE ARE HIS BETROTHED

Our bridegroom has gone away, but He will be back. John explains that this time of separation is also the time of preparation:

> *What we will be has not yet been made known. But we know that when he appears, we shall be like him, for we shall see him as he is. Everyone who has this hope in him purifies himself, just as he is pure.* (1 John 3:2b–3)

The Jewish wedding ceremony took place in three parts. Each part was symbolic of a much greater wedding. It began with the "betrothal," which was preceded by intense bargaining between the father of the bride and the father of the groom. The "bride price" was very steep. The price was comparable to what you might pay for a new house today. Then, when the bride price was paid, there was a ceremony in which the couple were "betrothed." The price Jesus paid for us, of course, was not silver or gold, but His precious blood. If we have put our trust in that blood, there is a ring on our finger. We are betrothed. In the days of Jesus, this part of the ceremony symbolized a permanent commitment.

Next, the groom went away in order to add a room to his father's house for his bride. It usually took about a year, but the actual length of time the groom was gone varied. It wasn't until the *father* said all was ready, the groom came back in a great processional with his friends, surprising the bride.

Jesus said,

> *In my Father's house are many rooms; if it were not so, I would have told you.*
> *I am going there to prepare a place for you. And if I go and prepare a place for you,*
> *I will come back and take you to be with me that you also may be where I am.*
> (John 14:2–3)

During this time of separation, the bride was preparing her wedding gown, the actual garment she would wear on that special day. It involved time and patience. It involved intricate detail. As we anticipate our great wedding day, we are preparing our "wedding gown." Rather than fine linens, our wedding gown is the purity of our character. Our character is developed as we clothe ourselves with the Lord Jesus Christ, as we live out the principles in 1 John. Everyone who has the hope of Jesus returning is in a process of sanctification. As he remains open to God, he purifies himself as He is pure. We are a work in progress. It takes time and patience. It takes diligence as we eagerly anticipate what we will become. What a day that will be! John was given a vision of that amazing day, which he recorded in the book of Revelation:

> *For the wedding of the Lamb has come,*
> *and his bride has made herself ready.*
> *Fine linen, bright and clean,*
> *was given her to wear.*
> *(Fine linen stands for the righteous acts of the saints.)* (Revelation 19:7b–8)

We are now God's betrothed in our "ball cap and jeans." We are getting ready to become His bride. Jesus has gone away to prepare a place for us. And He *will* be back. It will be a great and wondrous processional.

> *All glorious is the princess within her chamber;*
> *her gown is interwoven with gold.*
> *In embroidered garments she is led to the king.*
> (Psalm 45:13–14a)

There is so much symbolism here. Let's just paraphrase this verse a little bit. Kathy read it to me this way:

> *All glorious is Kathy within her chamber;*
> *her character is interwoven with gold.*
> *In embroidered garments she is led to Jesus.*

The words that are used here are significant. We've often talked about what suffering and "picking up one's cross" produce in the heart of a woman. The fires of life will refine and purify your character into a magnificent gold if you allow God to use them as He desires. Many of us know women who already "glisten" with the attributes of God. When you embroider, you enhance, you magnify, you add color. So read this verse again as you insert your name:

> *All glorious is _____ within her chamber; the character of*
> *God is interwoven throughout her character. Clothed in the many-splendored col-*
> *ors of love, she is led to Jesus.*

The third part of the Jewish marriage involved the actual wedding and wedding feast. The celebration lasted seven days. Oh, what rejoicing there will be in heaven at the ultimate wedding banquet!

So in this period of separation, God yearns to sanctify us and make us holy. It is His heart's desire. Let's continue to abandon ourselves to Him.

> *Everyone who has this hope in him purifies himself, just as he is pure.* (1 John 3:3)

YOU AIN'T DA SAME WOMAN

We've had a lot of laughs talking about our "wedding weekend" in Atlanta. Kathy got razzed about how she walked down the aisle, and about her transformation from grunge to glamour. We didn't know it would be such a perfect analogy for this book. When she was walking out of her hotel room one morning, prepared to sing and to speak, the maid called down the hall to her.

> "S'cuse me. S'cuse me." She moved closer. "You ain't da same woman I saw yestaday—are ya?"
>
> I smiled at her inquisitiveness. I knew I looked different. "Yes, I certainly am."

If you know Jesus, if you have put your trust in what He did for you on the cross, the process has begun. You are in the betrothal period. You are now getting ready for your Bridegroom's return. The true and eternal transformation will *not* happen with makeup, surgery, or wardrobe—it will happen because of His life being poured into you: more of His light, more of His truth, more of His mercy. This is the only way it will happen. As His bride, we can be bought and transformed by no other means.

Before we look individually at the principles that will pour His life into us, we must make sure that you understand the only way you can become His betrothed.

THERE'S POWER IN THE BLOOD

We all know parents who want their children to grow up to be loving men and women, men and women of character, but who absolutely would not want their children to be taught about the depravity of man or the blood of Christ. Yet the only way we can be redeemed from the "empty way of life handed down" by our forefathers, is through the blood of the Lamb (1 Peter 1:18–19).

(Dee) I remember taking a new neighbor to Bible study. While the women met, their preschool children were in the corresponding Bible club.

My neighbor was quiet on the way home, but her daughter was singing enthusiastically in the backseat:

> *What can wash away my sin?*
> *Nothing but the blood of Jesus.*
> *What can make me whole again?*
> *Nothing but the blood of Jesus.*
> *O precious is the flow*
> *That makes me white as snow*
> *No other fount I know*
> *Nothing but the blood of Jesus.*

My neighbor became as still and as cold as an ice sculpture. When we got to her house and her little girl bounded out of the car and ran up the walk, she turned to me and said evenly:

> "I can't believe that Amy was exposed to something so gruesome.
> I know you meant well, Dee, but this is not for us. We will not be back."

I grieved over her response. I was saddened that her child was going to be kept from learning more about Jesus. I thought about what Paul wrote:

> *For the message of the cross is foolishness to those who are perishing, but to us who are being saved it is the power of God.* (1 Corinthians 1:18)

And yet I also understood my neighbor's reaction. God's most wonderful mysteries can seem very strange: the way of His mercy falling on our cold hearts, the way prepared for us for eternal life . . . and even the way of a man with a woman. I remember exactly where I was when I first heard about the mystery of sex, because I was so stunned. I was twirling around on the swings during recess with my best friend, Donna Rosenow, when she told me how babies were made. I thought she was trying to play a trick on me, to see how gullible I could be. If I swallowed this story, then she would laugh at me. But she was my best friend, and generally not one to play mean tricks. Donna said, "My *mother* told me. She's a Christian and she wouldn't lie."

Could it be? I struggled to believe it, and it didn't seem beautiful at all. I decided right then and there all my children would be adopted. Yet there came a time when I realized the wonder of this truth, the beauty of the sexual relationship, and the great mystery of God's plan to make a husband and a wife one.

(Kathy) In the same way, I had the veil completely lifted from my eyes when I first grasped what Jesus did for me on the cross. Crucifixes were so much a part of my environment growing up. My family had them hanging over the headboards in most of the bedrooms. Some were even on the tops of dressers with candles around them. As a child I rarely saw adults without a crucifix around their necks. It wasn't just the cross, it was the full body of Jesus in agony.

Even at church when I'd focus on the huge crucifix above the altar I was numb to the sight of it all. I had seen it so often: the crown of thorns, the blood trickling down His face, the bleeding wound in His side, the nails in His hands and feet. It all just seemed like some great tragedy from a Shakespearean play. I was removed from it because I didn't understand what it really had to do with *my* life. Yet a time came when I realized the significance of what Jesus did on the cross. I wept on and off for several months. My heart was pierced with the knowledge of Christ and what He had done for me. I would never be the same again. I understood the true meaning of His death, the great mystery of God's plan to reconcile me with Himself. The cross became sacred.

ILLUMINATION

For all of us who have come to know Jesus, there came a time when we saw the light. For some it was a glimpse of light, like a little crack in the door when a parent checks on a child in the middle of the night. For some of us it was as startling as when floodlights are turned on within a dark stadium. Whether slowly or suddenly, we eventually came to the point where the light penetrated deep into the darkness of our souls and illuminated Jesus clearly. We came to understand who He is and who we are. As a matter of fact, even as you are reading this, people are experiencing "the light going on" all over the world. It will continue to happen as it has happened in the past because Jesus is on a continual pursuit for His beloved, to make them His betrothed.

Consider how it happened for the author of 1 John. Come with us on a brief but wondrous journey. With the help of paintings from the Masters, consider how God moved John, and his fisherman friend, Simon Peter, from bumbling fishermen to mighty men of God.

When did Peter and John become "His"? At what point did the light come on? Perhaps it was when Jesus called to them and they left their nets to follow Him. Perhaps it was when they confessed their faith. Maybe it was when they saw the risen Lord. By the time John writes his letter, there is a breathless excitement about knowing Jesus. John begins his letter almost as if he is running from the empty tomb.

> *I myself have seen him with my own eyes . . .*
> *I have touched him with my own hands.*
> (1 John 1:1b TLB)

Peter has the same euphoria in his letters:

> *For we have not been telling you fairy tales . . .*
> *My own eyes have seen his splendor and his glory.*
> (2 Peter 1:16 TLB)

There is no doubt, that by this time, they are His betrothed.

THE CRACK IN THE DOOR

Can you even imagine seeing the things they saw firsthand, being in the actual presence of Jesus as He wooed them to Himself?

The first encounter they had with Him occurred after they had been fishing all night and had caught nothing. When Jesus told them to let down their nets on the other side, the fish were so plentiful that their nets began to break. Peter fell at the knees of Jesus and said,

Go away from me, Lord; I am a sinful man! (Luke 5:8)

THE MIRACULOUS
DRAUGHT
OF FISHES

RAPHAEL (1483–1520)

Surely this was the crack in the door. The light made Peter see how "big" Jesus was and how "little" he was. He felt exposed. He must have wondered, *Oh my—who is this?* From the very beginning, when they left their nets to follow Jesus, they *knew* Jesus was different, yet they did not comprehend, at first, that He *truly* was God incarnate.

A WIDENING LIGHT

Remember when they were out in a storm with Him? They were terrified of the waves and the lightning. The Sea of Galilee is capable of great fury, and the waves, we are told, threatened to overturn the boat.

In their panic they awakened Jesus. They called on Jesus to do *something*. Surely this great Man could pray—He seemed to have such a connection with the Father. Or surely He could give them instructions so the boat would not sink—He seemed so very wise.

CHRIST IN THE STORM
ON THE SEA OF GALILEE

REMBRANDT, PAINTED IN 1633

Instead, Jesus did what He often does—He responds in ways that make us stand in awe of Him, causing us to realize that we are dealing with God Almighty. He stood up and told the sea to be calm. Can you even imagine?

Seeing the turbulent sea transformed to a placid lake stunned the disciples. They seemed even more frightened than they had been of the storm. They looked at one another, asking:

> *What kind of man is this? Even the winds and the waves obey him!*
> (Matthew 8:27)

Jesus continued to illuminate their souls concerning who He was and why He came. They watched Him give sight to the blind, raise the dead, feed the multitudes, and finally, conquer death.

MY LORD AND MY GOD

In the beginning of John's letter, not only does he say he has heard and seen Christ, but his hands have touched Him! It reminds us of John's account of Thomas. When Thomas doubted, Jesus said: "Put your finger here; see my hands. Reach out your hand and put it into my side. Stop doubting and believe" (John 20:27). Thomas responds, "My Lord and my God!" (John 20:28). Notice in this painting how Caravaggio shows that several other disciples were just as curious as Thomas!

DOUBTING
THOMAS
—————
CARAVAGGIO
(1573–1610)

The risen Jesus was not a figment of their imagination. Jesus was not just a charismatic leader. He was God. "The Word became flesh and dwelt among us," John says (John 1:14 NKJV). His heart was still full of amazement as it pulsed through his writings. Charles Spurgeon reminds us of who John was:

Remember what order of man John was, that disciple whom Jesus loved, whose head had leaned on Jesus' bosom . . . This is he who at one time saw

ST. JOHN

TITIAN, 1535

the pierced heart of the well-beloved pouring forth blood and water; and at another beheld the Lion of the tribe of Judah prevail to take the book and loose the seven seals thereof. [1]

Surely the apostles had an experience with Jesus that we have not had. Still, you don't have to have lived when Jesus walked the earth in order to *know* that He is God, that He will walk hand in hand with you, and that He *will* turn your whole world around.

(*Dee*) I came to Christ as a young wife and mother. I had no idea that I had been living in darkness, blinded by my selfishness. All I knew was that the life I had wanted, and was getting, left me feeling empty. I was sad and

I was angry. I was blaming other people. I've even shared the fact that I threw a pan at my husband, saying, "You are not meeting my needs!"

Recently, I stepped into an elevator in a city hotel. Another woman was already inside, and as the doors closed, she surprised me by asking,

"How big a pan was it?"

I was the only other one in the elevator, so I knew she was talking to me. "Pardon me?"

"The pan. I read how you threw a pan at your husband . . . You seem so quiet, so gentle."

"Oh . . ." I flushed, realizing she had recognized me. "Well, I wasn't so gentle before Jesus."

"Really? That surprises me," she said. "Well, anyhow, how big was the pan?"

I laughed. I tried to remember. "It was so long ago—thirty-five years. I really can't remember."

"Was it a skillet?"

I laughed again at her persistence, feeling like I was on candid camera. I was glad no one else was in the elevator. "Honestly, I can't recall. I'm just thankful I missed."

"I'm glad too," she said. "Your husband sounds so nice."

As I walked to my hotel room, my heart was filled with memories. How thankful I am that God was so patient and loving with me in my immaturity. I learned that my misery had not been my husband's fault at all. As I understood what it meant to step out of my own darkness and walk in God's light it became very clear to me what needed to change—not my husband, not my surroundings, but me.

When we remember the early days of illumination, we are grateful. But it is vital that we don't live on memories. It is vital that we keep stretching ourselves to trust Him, daily, the way we did in the beginning. If we get out of the light and live only on memories, we become what Oswald Chambers describes as sentimental Christians. If that is true of you, Chambers says,

. . . your testimony will have a hard metallic ring to it. Beware of trying to cover up your present refusal to "walk in the light" by recalling your past experiences when you did "walk in the light." [2]

PRECIOUS AS GOLD

Though you are His betrothed, your wedding gown is not ready. The Father is eager to present you as a radiant bride to His Son and to embroider your gown with the colors of His love. You may remember that we could not list all the colors of God's love. But we *can* tell you that Scripture often uses gold to represent the best and the most beautiful of all of God's colors, and the psalmist tells us that as we grow in holiness, the Lord will embroider our wedding gowns with gold. We can also, on the basis of the opening of John's letter, tell you *three* of the threads of gold with which God will embroider your wedding gown, *if* you obey the principles of 1 John.

THE THREADS OF GOLD

Gold Thread #1: True Intimacy with the Father and with Jesus
We proclaim to you what we have seen and heard,
so that you also may have fellowship with us.
And our fellowship is with the Father
and with his Son, Jesus Christ.
(1 John 1:3)

When you live in continual repentance, God purifies you so that there is nothing between you and Him, and you can experience the joy of His presence. You see, sin will not cut off your *relationship* with God, but it will hurt your *fellowship* with Him. But if all is clean, when you wake in the morning, He is there—when you curl up with your Bible and your coffee, He puts wonder in your soul with revelations. When you move through your day, interacting with people, you see them through His eyes. There is hope in your heart, gladness in your step, for your Bridegroom is by your side, guiding you, loving you.

By the time John writes his letter, this is his experience. Do you remember how immature John and his brother James had been as young disciples? They wanted assurance of the best seats in heaven. Their thoughts were all about themselves. But John has been purified, and he is truly a holy man. He is experiencing true intimacy, and he longs for us to know the same.

(Kathy) I have been asking God lately to make me not just a Christian woman, but a holy woman. Like you, I can fall into a place of complacency. I think it's somewhat easier to live under the label of Christian than to live under the label of holy. Mediocrity often fights for the throne in our lives. When I looked up the synonyms for *mediocre*, this is what I found:

"average, second-rate, fair, indifferent, moderate, so-so"

Yuck! Who wants to live a life that falls under those headings? Who wants to be a bride that is described that way? We would hate it if people said, "Oh, Kathy Troccoli and Dee Brestin—they are such average women. Ever hang around them? They're just so-so."

In one reference to the word *mediocre*, I read, "unexceptional." That really made my skin crawl. So many of us live with a banner over us. It reads:

Ordinary
Unexceptional
Just plain blah . . .

We must not settle. We have access to His power. We can continually drink from the river of His love. Why don't we take advantage of this? He will take us to higher and greater places if we would trust Him to do so and make ourselves available to Him. That's when your banner will read differently:

Ordinary becomes *extraordinary.*
Unexceptional becomes *exceptional.*
Just plain blah becomes *a woman transformed.*

How? It's the Jesus in you.

Don't let the cares of the day, the stresses of the moments, and the worries of tomorrow interfere with your communing and partaking of the love affair that Jesus longs for you to have with Him. Don't live your Christianity by "going through the motions"—acting like, sounding like, and being like a Christian. That's why so many of us give without joy, talk without grace, and live without peace.

We have talked about how personal, how intimate our God can be, surprising you, speaking to you directly through His Word or through His Spirit. Wouldn't you love to have moments, each day, when God *surprises* you, the way a bridegroom surprises his bride-to-be?

(Dee) During our weekend in Atlanta, one young woman came up to me after I spoke on Mary of Bethany. She had tears in her eyes and said,

> "Dee, I didn't know what you were going to speak about—I hadn't read your book. I didn't know you were going to explain why Mary of Bethany had such an intimate and wonderful relationship with Jesus. I have to show you what I prayed."

> She showed me her prayer journal. It was open to October 18—just the preceding day. To the best of my memory, this is a summary of what she had written:

> *Precious Lord—how I long to be like Mary of Bethany, sitting at Your feet, drinking in Your words. Please reveal to me what caused her to have the heart she did. You found great delight in her. Please bring me higher, Lord. Help me to be open to whatever You have for me.*

Her face was radiant. "He certainly kissed me tonight with His presence, didn't He?"

The Lord is so wonderful like that. He longs to embroider our gowns with true intimacy with Him. How it pleases Him when we seek this.

Gold Thread #2: True Intimacy with One Another
If we walk in the light, as he is in the light,
we have fellowship with one another. (1 John 1:7a)

John promises that when our fellowship with the Father is genuine and real, we will not only have true intimacy with God, but true intimacy with one another. This is one of the strongest themes of John's letter. The mark of a Christian is Christ's love: love for our neighbor and, *especially*, love for our sisters and brothers in Christ. For if our fellowship with God is real, we are going to reflect His heart toward others. We are also going to be knit to those who are experiencing that same intimacy with God. We are going to be delighted in the Christ we see in them. Charles Spurgeon helps us to understand:

> *In our fellow-men, there may be something loveable; but in our fellow-Christians, there must be something loveable. . . . I hardly know of a more beautiful sight than a newborn Christian. I like to hear the prayer of the one who is just converted; there may be much of mistake and imperfection in it, but that does not spoil it. ...There is nothing more lovely to be seen in the whole world than an aged believer, who has lived very near to God.* [3]

If we cannot show love for others, both for our neighbor and for our brothers and sisters in the Lord, it is a red flag that something is very wrong in our relationship with God. Perhaps without even realizing it, we have slipped into the shadows.

*(Dee)*When I look back to the beginning of my marriage, it surely was a rocky road. But it's been thirty-six years since I said "yes" to Steve, and our relationship has become *so* sweet. People have trouble believing how good it is. (They may think I'm kind of sappy about it.) And it didn't happen overnight. As a matter of fact, one woman keeps writing reviews of my books for Amazon.com and calling me a "Stepford Wife." "Nobody," she writes emphatically, "has that great a marriage." I just sigh and smile because what she doesn't understand is that the power of God can transform any relation-

ship if we allow Him access to our hearts. It takes work. It takes dying to self. It takes a continual falling at the feet of Jesus and remaining vulnerable, teachable, and repentant.

I learned in those early years that when there was trouble between Steve and me, there was trouble between Jesus and me. I had to get alone with God so He could tell me what the true problem was. You know what? He always did. And most times, *I* was the problem. It always managed to take my relationship with Steve to a higher level. I am so thankful that Steve pursues the heart of God, and I know I am blessed because of that. I have no doubt that it is often easier to show love to a believing husband than to an unbelieving one. (My heart grieves for women married to hardhearted men, for sometimes it seems impossible for their mates to be at peace with them. The light in a godly wife makes a hardhearted and foolish husband rage, for it exposes his darkness. How we need to pray for tenderness of heart in unbelieving husbands, so that the light in his wife will cause him to repent!) But whatever the state of your mate's heart, your ability to love him will be profoundly affected by your own intimacy with God.

(*Kathy*) Even though I am single, I have rich and fulfilling relationships. I work very hard to maintain them, even though life can be extremely hectic. What Dee just talked about concerning her relationship with Steve is the same process that occurs in my friendships. If there is tension in communication, or misunderstandings, or a flareup, I must go to God for wisdom about the situation. He not only gives me insight, but His light penetrates my darkness, illuminating the things I don't want to see in myself. No one wants to be uncovered. And yet it is God's desire to expose our true hearts so that we can have His true heart. When that happens, our relationships with one another become pure and sweet.

As women, we are the relational sex. We care about making our friendships and our marriages work. (It isn't that men do *not* care. It is just that generally speaking, we women define ourselves by our relationships, so when our closest relationships break down, we are heartsick.) Learning to walk in the light will embroider our wedding gowns with the gold of sweet, intimate fellowship.

Gold Thread #3: Our Joy Will Be Complete
We are writing these things so that our joy may be complete.
(1 John 1:4 NRSV)

Can you even imagine having a joy that is complete? We know vacations lift our spirits, that the first daffodils pushing up through the frozen earth gladden our hearts, and a newborn baby puts a smile on everyone's face. But have we ever experienced a continuous *full* feeling of joy? Life is hard and some of us just barely get glimpses of happiness. So many holes in our hearts need to be filled. We long for hope, we long for peace, we long to belong, and we long to feel at home. Many of us have known Jesus for years and still have that all too familiar "deep ache." Jesus tells us that in this world we will have trouble, and we do. Yet John says fellowship with the Father and the Son will make our joy *complete*. So if it does not mean freedom from trouble, what does it mean?

Living in *complete joy* requires living in *complete confidence* in God. Each day can have a little more peace than yesterday, last month, or even a year ago, because though we still have sorrow, our joy is inextinguishable when we completely trust the heart of our Bridegroom.

Psalm 16 gives us a picture of the complete joy John is promising as we cultivate intimacy with God.

> *The boundary lines have fallen for me in pleasant places;*
> *surely I have a delightful inheritance.* (Psalm 16:6)

This does not mean that life is free of pain, problems, and PMS. No doubt, right now, you are experiencing problems in your life. We are! Complete joy is not about our circumstances. Complete joy is about confidence in the Bridegroom's love and purposes for us. We have hope in every valley for we know that, in His time, the boundary lines will be pleasant and the inheritance delightful. Even in the midst of enormous pain, we discover we can trust God and His way is perfect because we know:

LORD, you have assigned me my portion and my cup;
you have made my lot secure. (Psalm 16:5)

And though we will still know suffering, though our constantly changing circumstances can cause pain, underneath is an unchanging joy. The psalmist goes on to promise that as you set the Lord always before you, you will not be shaken. That brings a divine confidence, which brings a divine peace, which opens wide the window to let in a divine joy.

Our joy becomes more complete as we learn to watch our affections, our addictions, and our compulsions. We were created to worship God. If we're not worshiping Him, we will worship something else. If the true "affections of our heart" are not toward God, they will be toward something else. That something else is bound to drag us down. "The sorrows of those will increase who run after other gods" (Psalm 16:4), so we must keep ourselves from idols (1 John 5:21). Throughout His Word the Lord was very specific when He talked about idols. He knew that they could easily steal the affections of the heart. So often He not only asked His people to break them but to crush them into powder.

We must continue to daily place His words of life in our hearts so that we might not sin against Him (Psalm 119:11). His Word is a protection from deception. We must take that time alone with the Lord to read and pray on His Word so that He can continue to reveal Himself over the chaos in our everyday lives. Only with that kind of daily intimacy will we be able to experience the complete joy the psalmist describes:

You have made known to me the path of life;
you will fill me with joy in your presence,
with eternal pleasures at your right hand. (Psalm 16:11)

Wouldn't you love to have these threads of gold on your "wedding gown," these threads of a greater intimacy with God, a sweeter relationship with one another, and a more complete joy?

ESTHER: CLOTHED IN THE MANY-SPLENDORED COLORS OF HIS LOVE

Later in this book we will look at the story of Esther, who is a wonderful illustration of all that John is teaching. Esther became a beautiful bride, her gown embroidered with the gold John is describing.

The Esther we remember was beautiful, and the way her story is often told, it seems she was perfect! But when we look very carefully at Esther's life, you may be surprised. You may know there was a beauty contest in the book of Esther, but did you know it involved sleeping with the king? You may know that Esther hid her faith, but did you know that she hid it for seven years, and that to do so she probably had to eat unkosher food and participate in idol worship? We will show you that Esther and the other believers in the story did not take the highest road in the beginning of the story, but as the story progresses, there is true repentance. Esther does become a radiant bride.

Our God is a God of second chances. Esther learns to walk in the light, to die to herself, to live by the truth, and to show mercy to her brother. As she does this, her "wedding gown" becomes adorned with threads of gold.

We are now ready to look closely at the four primary principles that can transform us into the likeness of Christ. The principles of 1 John are rooted in the power of

> *Light*
> *Death*
> *Truth*
> *Mercy*

As you learn how to live out these principles, you will be transformed into a radiant believer who bears the imprint of Christ, the colors of His glorious love.

The first principle has to do with light.

LIGHT

There is a lot of mystery to God. Many questions remain unanswered. As in Genesis, darkness still hovers over the earth and in our hearts and minds at times. But in that same account, God said, "Let there be light." He can, every day, speak that same command over us. That's how it begins. Though darkness hovers over us, God speaks:

Let there be light.

PRINCIPLE ONE:
TRANSFORMED
by LIGHT

*GOD IS LIGHT and no shadow of
darkness can exist in him.*
(1 JOHN 1:5B PHILLIPS)

This is the verdict: Light has come into the world, but men
loved darkness instead of light because their deeds were evil.

(JOHN 3:19)

CHAPTER 4

WALKING IN THE DARK

(Kathy)

Recently I drove by an art shop in Nashville. Seeing the easels set up outside the door caused me to fantasize about expressing myself with a paintbrush. I imagined wearing a beret, sitting on a terraced hill in Italy overlooking the vineyards. The sun would be setting and a cool breeze would be drying the masterpiece I had just created.

In the days that followed I tossed around the idea of expressing myself through painting. Before I knew it, I found myself back at that art shop. Like a child in a toy store, I stepped in with wide-eyed anticipation and quickly became intimidated by all I saw. I found myself faced with not only thousands of colors, but choices of mediums: pastels, acrylics, and oils. I had no idea what I was looking for. I saw big easels, small easels, fat easels, and skinny easels. I thought I might just start with buying the coolest-looking easel. (Yes, I'm a deep soul . . .)

Actually, atmosphere means everything to me. I quickly knew I was in way over my head and out of my element. It felt just like when my mother enrolled me in ballet class. She would drag me off the ball field, put me in the car, and talk excitedly about the recital at the end of the year. (What

57

excited *me* about it was that the recital meant the end of dance lessons until the fall.) Every week I arrived with a stomachache. I saw sweet little girls and sweet little outfits. And there *I* was—the tomboy in the tutu.

My mother finally came to her senses when her greatly anticipated recital night came along. She invited some of our relatives, including my grandma Troccoli. Because I never practiced, I never learned the dance routine. I was about to be handed over to the lions. The curtain opened. There I was, paralyzed, a human mannequin. *What could I do to prove I was real?* I started shuffling my feet. In years to come my mother would recall the remark from Grandma Troccoli that became my salvation:

"Whatsa matta witha Katalena?"

My mother knew there and then that her dream was my nightmare. Praise God from whom all blessings flow.

A store clerk in the art shop awakened me from my childhood memory.

"Need some help?"

"Yeah, actually I do. I want to paint. I don't have any idea what I'm doing. I don't know where to start. I'm clueless about what I need."

She kindly patted my arm and said, "Oh, honey, I know. You're looking for a creative outlet, aren't you?"

"Yes." I chuckled to myself, thinking, *Yeah, like I need one more creative outlet.*

IN THE BEGINNING

I may not understand much about painting, but there are a few principles of color I do understand. Black is dark and white is light. Are you impressed?

Seriously, darkness, in the physical world, is the absence of light. Scripture makes this point repeatedly. Just as this is true in the physical realm, so it is true in the spiritual realm. In the beginning of the world, and in the beginning of each of our lives, there was darkness.

In the opening of Genesis we are told:

Darkness was over the surface of the deep. (Genesis 1:2b)

Get that picture in your mind. It was completely black. Darkness has long been associated with evil, with frightening monsters in the night, spooky things: bats, spiders, and muggers in dark alleys. It has long been associated with Satan and with sin.

But the power of our Creator transformed it all.

God said, "Let there be light." (Genesis 1:3a)

In the same way, darkness resided in you and me before His light penetrated that darkness. David writes:

Surely I was sinful at birth,
*   sinful from the time my mother conceived me.* (Psalm 51:5)

Those who say that you have to be *taught* to be selfish, unkind, and dishonest must never have spent much time with toddlers. Even toddlers born into loving homes quite naturally rip their toys from their astonished baby sister's hands and lie with ease when asked about her tears. Darkness is the natural state of our hearts from the beginning.

Sibling rivalry is not the exception, but the rule. It is quite predictable that Baby Number One will be clingy, will revert to wetting his pants, and will find ways to express his rivalry when Baby Number Two infringes on his territory. His whole world has been rocked. His parents' love and attention are now divided, as if a dark cloud has moved in, blocking much of the sun's warmth. Author Adrianne Rich wrote: "When my sister was born, it was like losing the Garden of Eden."[1] Dee and I were the babies in our families, so we each have tales of being the victims of rivalry.

(Dee) I was about five and my big sisters were baby-sitting for me. I was pestering them while they were playing Monopoly. They told me to dial the "0" on the telephone and ask the woman who answered if the Easter Bunny was real. I ran off to do as I'd been told.

The operator didn't find it amusing. She lectured me severely, saying I was tying up the line when there could be a *real* emergency. Surprised by her anger, I went wailing back to my sisters:

"She got really, really mad. She told me never to do that again."

"Dee Dee," Bonnie said sternly, "You are in *big* trouble. I think the police might come and put you in jail."

Sally looked out the window, as if expecting the police. "You better hide behind the sofa. Bonnie and I will keep a lookout."

While I huddled behind the sofa for hours, finally falling asleep, my sisters enjoyed an uninterrupted game of Monopoly.

(Kathy) My rivalry included my six cousins. My sister and I played with them all the time. We all grew up together with our houses next to each other and our backyards joined. We had a big extended family consisting of my grandparents and my mom's two sisters and their families. The Troccolis, the Espositos, the Pellechias, and the Gallellis—we were our own little Italy on a corner in Long Island. Go ahead and laugh if you want. I know it sounds like a scene from *The Godfather*. In fact I have a little story for you . . .

I was sitting on a stool, center stage, at an event for women. It was shortly after my aunt Woolie died of breast cancer. I was explaining some of the things that transpired between us before she died. It was very emotional for me. The week before she passed away, I had time alone with her, to talk with her and to pray over her. I was so thankful that she prayed with me to invite Jesus into her heart.

As I explained the scene, I began crying in front of the audience. I was caught up in explaining what happened at her funeral—how her son Rico and I were standing in front of her casket, and I had reassured him that this was just his mother's shell. I told him of how we had had a beautiful talk, and I knew she was alive with Jesus. Rico was so comforted by what I had told him that he called Carmine, Dominick, Anthony, and Alfonse over to tell them his mother was alive in heaven! In the midst of my intensely poignant story, I could tell the women were suppressing their laughter. The names that

I rattled off so easily were so foreign to them. They were trying to be respectful because they could see how serious this was. I ended up just saying,

"Go ahead and laugh."

They broke up.

Then I continued with my story.

Anyhow, back to the rivalry. It extended to my Italian cousins. I played and fought with them the way most people do with their siblings. We were always having territorial fights:

Whose yard got to have the pup tent?

Who got to wear the Batman cape?

Who got to use the hammer to build the fort?

Who got to have the first hot dog off the grill?

I wasn't exempt from the pushing and shoving kids do to each other, but I knew, and I'd been told, that I had a sharp tongue. Once when Carmine and I were about seven, I was yelling at him and he ended up slugging me right in the face. I ran off screaming, flinging open doors, searching for my mother, saying:

"Carmine hit me! Carmine hit me!"

He followed me into the kitchen, wanting to defend himself.

"She was saying nasty things to me!"

My mom said: "Well, use your mouth like she does, not your fists!"

Later that afternoon I said something Carmine didn't like. He came over to me and bit my arm as hard as he could, leaving gigantic teeth marks in my skin. I ran home again, screaming to my mother:

"Carmine bit me! Carmine bit me!"

My mother was so angry. She came out looking for him. "What are you doing? Why did you bite her?"

"You told me to use my mouth!" Carmine replied defensively.

We could all tell tales of childhood rivalry. "Folly," Proverbs tells us, "is bound up in the heart of a child" (Proverbs 22:15a). Most parents address that foolishness. If a parent does not address it, sometimes someone else will step up to the plate. Most siblings, as they mature, put away these childish ways and learn how to live more harmoniously with each other.

But for some, the rivalry is never put aside. Weeds are meant to be pulled out when they are little. If they are not, they quickly flourish into ugly plants and vines that choke the beauty, the image of God, from our lives. No longer are the stories funny, but tragic.

Do Not Be Like Cain

That is what happened with Adam and Eve's firstborn son, Cain. As a matter of fact, "raising Cain" has come to mean causing trouble for no good reason. Cain's name has become synonymous with sin and darkness. He is the antithesis of the imprint of Christ—instead of reflecting Christ, he reflects the face of the evil one who was given free reign in his heart. Cain was *not* a believer, for John says he belonged to the evil one. But don't assume that because you *are* a believer, you are immune from being overpowered by sin. John's letter was written to believers, and he warns believers: "Do not be like Cain" (1 John 3:12a).

What was Cain's sin? *The answer is vital.* He refused the light of God time and time again. It is a fearful thing to wander from the light, because we can wander so far into darkness that we no longer hear God's gracious voice calling us, giving us new chances to return to the light. It happened to Cain and it can happen to us. Consider the dark, downward path Cain took and look at the chances God provided for Cain to turn back to Him.

Chance # 1: Choose to Stay in the Light

The story begins with Cain and Abel each bringing an offering to the Lord. Abel was operating on faith, and brought the best, a blood sacrifice, the firstborn of his flock. But instead of bringing the best, Cain chose something less precious, an offering of fruits and vegetables. And we are told:

> The LORD looked with favor on Abel and his offering, but on Cain and his offering he did not look with favor. (Genesis 4:4b–5a)

There was a reason that God asked for a blood sacrifice. It was the foreshadowing of the ultimate sacrifice.

THE BOUND LAMB

FRANCISO DE ZURBARAN
(ABOUT 1598–1664)

Cain's sin was not that he brought fruits and vegetables, but that he disobeyed God. *He chose to do it his way.* Cain was not listening to God. He had a chance to please Him, but he blew it, because he chose to do it his way. I don't think there's a person who cannot relate to this. Especially when the Bible may not go on and on to explain things to our liking. Sometimes the answer from God our Father is short and simple:

Because I said so.

That should be enough because He is God. However, many times His authority is not enough to motivate us to obedience. It may not make sense to us, for example, to refrain from premarital sex or to forgive a person who has genuinely hurt us. But when we do it our way, we find ourselves bearing the fruit of our choices. It may take a day, a month, or years—but outside the wisdom of God, we'll find ourselves with rotten fruit. Some of the darkest days on earth are recorded in the book of Judges. What was the reason for the depravity? "Every man did that which was right in his own eyes" (Judges 21:25b KJV).

In *The Divine Conspiracy*,[2] Dallas Willard tells of a pilot practicing high-speed maneuvers in a fighter jet. She became disoriented—thinking she was flying up a steep ascent—and flew straight into the ground. Willard says people without God are like that: they become disoriented, unaware that they are "flying upside down," taking themselves and innocent passengers to their deaths.

If you don't believe the absolute truths of God, and instead live by your own truths, you become disoriented, yet still take the controls, not realizing you are headed toward destruction. Proverbs 14:12 says, "There is a way that seems right to a man, but in the end it leads to death." We absolutely need the light of God in order to walk in the ways of God and to enjoy the abundant and eternal life He's promised.

(Kathy) After I gave my life to Christ, I really had to change the template of how I processed right and wrong. If someone did me wrong, I wanted to do them wrong. If someone didn't like the way I was doing something, I thought, *Tough—that's your problem.* Now, because of the light of God exposing my darkness, all the rules have changed. My old rules looked nothing like God's rules.

Brick by brick, I had to start tearing *my* fortress down and rebuild—this time *God's* fortress. I needed to use His blueprint, His bricks, and His boundaries. I'll give you an example from my early years as a Christian. The light of God made me respond entirely differently than I would have if I had been operating in the dark.

I couldn't wait to go to church on Sunday when I first understood that I could have a relationship with Jesus. I loved learning about Him through the sermons. I loved singing the new hymns. I loved reading my Bible. My mom quickly grew increasingly worried about my "newfound faith." She didn't understand the whole "born-again thing." It was a separate religion to her. Here I was experiencing the greatest find of my life and my mom was heartsick that I was "joining some cult" and "being led astray."

I couldn't help but continue to have a passion in my heart to know everything I could know about Jesus. I found that I had a growing desire to be
baptized and to be immersed in water. I wanted to experience the whole
thing—the beautiful symbol of dying to the old way of life and coming up
a new creation: death, burial, and resurrection. I wanted to be baptized the
way I think Jesus was. I started to go to Friday night classes and offered to
sing a special song at the baptism. At this time in my life I was writing songs
almost every day about Jesus and my love for Him. My mom continued to
get upset. I knew she didn't understand.

Because my extended family was so close, and because my dad had died
when I was fifteen, my mother shared her apprehensions about my choices
with "the family." One night a couple of my uncles came over to talk to me.
It wasn't that they ever communicated that much with me, but now they had
a lot to say:

> "You're destroying your mother."
> "Isn't our church good enough for you?"
> "Your father's rolling over in his grave."
> "Stick to your own religion."

I remained silent. Deep down I knew that they were trying to "protect me."
How could they possibly understand? When they left, I thought long and hard
about the whole situation. Even then I had a sense that God was changing my
heart. It would have been typical of me to think and to say, "Too bad. You're
ignorant. You don't have a clue. I'm going to do what I want to do."

No person helped me sift through my thoughts. No person helped me
with my decision. The Spirit of God alone shed light into my soul. I felt like
He gave me the wisdom of His heart and the peace of His mind in this particular situation. I knew that I loved God and I knew He loved me. I wanted
so desperately to live for Him. Baptism is a way to honor Christ. I was sure
of my salvation whether I got baptized or not. But I also knew that God
commanded me to honor my mother and father. If this was going to put a
wedge between my mother and me, then I knew I should wait to get baptized. So I did.

I did go to the baptismal service. I did sing a song. I remember being teary about not being able to join everyone else, but I had such a calm in my soul that I was doing the right thing. A couple of days later I knew that my family would be inquisitive about what happened. My mother told them that I ended up not getting baptized. One aunt said, "But how do you really know that Kathleen didn't get baptized?" That really hurt because I knew why I came to make the choice I made, and they thought I was being deceptive. I had to trust that God would defend me. (This aunt, by the way, was my aunt Woolie, with whom I prayed in the hospital.)

I was able to make the choice I made because the Lord gave me the bigger picture. Sometimes He will do that if we really seek Him. Sometimes, especially as young believers, we can get a chip on our shoulder and think, *All of you are so spiritually ignorant. I'm just going to do what I need to do. I'm going to do what God told me to do.* Isn't it funny how often we blame God for the choices we make? We must be very careful when we say, "God said this to me or God told me to do this . . ." Most of the time this kind of talk is cloaked with our own agendas. I knew I had to wait and let my mother see the difference Jesus would make in my life. I thank God that I had the soberness of heart and that His Spirit gave me the fruit of patience and self-control to truly wait. God needed time to work in my mom's heart.

There is definitely a relationship between John's principle of walking in His light and walking in His love. God's light allowed me to see His path of love and to walk in it. And in time, He honored my obedience before my mother and my family.

I don't know exactly how this happened, but somehow, a number of years later, my mom got an "okay" from a Catholic priest. She got a written letter from him that I could be baptized. That is almost unheard of. Although my mother wasn't pleased with it, she gave me the choice. So I did get baptized. I really wanted my mom to come, but she didn't. Many women at the church rejoiced with me that night. They brought me precious little mementos because they knew it was a bittersweet experience.

When my mother got sick, her heart softened about many issues. She even apologized about some of the things we went through together. She understood more now. Facing death often has a way of helping us see what's important and what is not. Many realize then that it isn't about being in a particular denomination—it's about knowing Jesus. I'm thankful she finally saw that I was trying to be a better woman and do what God would want me to do.

If only I could make those choices all the time.

We *always* have a chance to choose God's way. Cain had that chance. But he chose his way and God was displeased. When the Lord looked with favor on Abel and his offering, but not on Cain and his offering, anger and depression welled up in Cain.

> *So Cain was very angry, and his face was downcast.*
> (Genesis 4:5b)

Isn't that like most of us? God asks us to do something, and we don't; then when we suffer a consequence, we get angry with Him. We can even get into a funk about it. Though sin is not the only cause for depression, it is one possible cause. So it is always wise to ask yourself, when you're down, if there is a particular sin in your life that is keeping out the joy and light of God.

Cain had disobeyed God, and now he was disheartened. Even though he had chosen his own way, God cared about his pain. When you are suffering because of bad choices, God doesn't condemn you, saying: *Well, kiddo, you deserve it. You made your bed, lie in it.* No. God cares for you. He comes to you and entreats you. The smartest thing in the world you can do at that point is swallow your pride and yield to the Spirit.

CHANCE # 2: RESPOND TO THE CONVICTION OF GOD

There are many reasons God may ask us questions. Sometimes it is to remind us of who He is. Sometimes it is to strengthen our faith. Sometimes it is to lead us to repentance. It is always to shed light on our path. How different is the Father of lights from the father of darkness.

(Kathy) I remember walking slowly through the Metropolitan Museum of Art in New York City, in awe of the talent God had bestowed upon man. I

stood before a painting of Adam and Eve, and shuddered at the ominous presence of evil in the serpent wrapped tightly around the tree. I could almost hear the conversation that happened that day in the Garden. "Did God *really* say?" "Are you sure?" How often *I* have been tempted to listen to those words. But Satan is always pulling a fast one. He wants us to doubt God. Why? So he can wreak havoc in our lives. So he can bring unimaginable pain into our days here on earth.

One of my favorite lines I have ever written is in a song called "At Your Mercy."

> *It only takes a moment's time for me to somehow cross the line*
> *where I can wind up roaming in the dark.*
> *Satan is a liar, I know he can start a fire*
> *then go tearing everything I have apart.*[3]

This line comes to me often, especially as God is allowing me the wonderful privilege of ministering more and more deeply to women. We must always weigh what our choices will do to the lives of other people. If we fall, what will be the consequences? We need to ask, *If I choose this, what will this do?* It would certainly be enlightening if God would throw out a heavenly scroll and list the pain that will come to us and to others. But though we may not know the specific pain, we certainly can see clearly what giving in to temptation has done in the lives of others. For example, throughout history sexual sin has attacked great men and women of God. It has always affected the whole of the church. Satan often appeals to our senses, for when they are allured, we have trouble thinking clearly. Instead of dwelling on the painful consequences that are likely to follow, we think only of the present pleasure.

How vital it is for us to think past the moment. If we allow ourselves to sit quietly under the light of God, His Spirit will plead with us. His questions, unlike the questions of the enemy, are only designed to help us, to draw us toward the light. If we would really trust God, then every day, we would gladly ask Him to search us and reveal His heart to us. Look at God's tenderness toward Cain, when He comes to him, gently, with a question:

Why are you angry? Why is your face downcast? (Genesis 4:6)

This is *so* significant: God gives Cain a choice. He can respond to God's light or he can refuse it. The direction he takes will have huge consequences, for good or for evil, for joy or for despair. This is what the Lord tells Cain:

> *Why is your face so dark with rage? It can be bright with joy if you will do what you should! But if you refuse to obey, watch out. Sin is waiting to attack you, longing to destroy you. But you can conquer it!* (Genesis 4:6b–7 TLB)

We have a choice. And that choice will either open the door to the Spirit flowing in, flooding our hearts with light and love, or it will open the door to the evil one, flooding our hearts with darkness, depression, and despair. The New International Version (NIV) says "sin is crouching at your door; it desires to have you . . ."

(Dee) After Steve and I had three children, God gave us the desire to adopt from overseas orphanages. The first daughter we adopted was Annie, a precious five-year-old from an orphanage in Seoul. Our twelve-year-old daughter, Sally, was thrilled that she was going to finally have a sister—that is, until the day Annie arrived. Sally remembers the day:

> *I had been the baby of the family for twelve years, and the only girl, and the center of attention.*
>
> *I was excited to have a sister. I was excited to have somebody to play with. But as soon as this adorable little doll with shiny black hair walked off the plane, I saw all the attention suddenly shift from me to her.*
>
> *"This isn't good," I thought to myself.*
>
> *My heart began to change. I let envy take hold of me. I became jealous, depressed, and sad. I really didn't love my new sister and I was very angry with her. She bugged me. I didn't want to talk to her. I didn't want to be with her. Misery was my state of heart for four or five months.*

I remember that time so well. A complete romantic, I had imagined Sally and Annie sharing the same bedroom, giggling under the covers, like the sisters in *Little House on the Prairie* or *Little Women*. Instead, Sally, who had been so sunny before, became dark and withdrawn. She began to lose weight and was having trouble sleeping. She didn't want to share a room with Annie. She even said, "Her breathing bugs me."

I told Sally: "You are *so* loved. You are absolutely adored. But you have this frightened little sister who cannot even speak English and who desperately needs your love." There were times when I nearly lost it, because I wanted to yell, "What is the matter with you? Just snap out of it, Sally!"

My spiritual gift is that of a prophet, who longs to tell the truth—but truth needs to be balanced with mercy. Thank God for my husband, who *does* have the spiritual gift of mercy.

Steve told me, "You wouldn't tell someone who has the flu to 'Snap out of it.' You can't do that to Sally either. This is huge for her. She needs our love and understanding." Steve would sit next to Sally's bed for hours at night, stroking her hair, singing hymns, telling her of our love, and praying for her. Sally remembers how God began to entreat her:

> One night our family went to a Christian concert, and afterwards one of the singers stepped forward. He talked about Jesus and His love for us. He said, "When you feel like you've got a sin that's controlling your life, give it to the Lord. Tell Him you're wrong, ask for forgiveness, and He'll cleanse you from it. He has the power to change you."
>
> I knew there was this "yuck" in my life, this gross stuff, this envy, this jealousy, this sadness. I seemed powerless to get rid of it and I didn't know what to do. I was so frustrated. I knew it was wrong, but I didn't know how to love my sister. So I just said, "God, I just need You to change me. I need You to take this from me. I'm so sorry. You know I can't do this. I can't love her. I can't get rid of this jealousy. I'm so mad at her. Just take this away, please, and give me some of Your love to give to her."
>
> You know what? That was the turning point for me. God began to change my perception of my sister. I went home and it was as if God had given me new eyes for my sister. She was no longer a competitor for my parents' love. I began to see that my parents loved me too, just as much. And I began to see her as now a hurting child who not only desperately needed the love of my parents, but she also needed the love of her sister.
>
> God gave me a love for her that was definitely not my own. Since then things

have just gotten so much better. The following year we really became close. It was a slow process and sometimes I did struggle with envy, but the Lord really did change my heart.

We could see a definite change in Sally's attitude, but Sally was still struggling with sleeplessness and irritability. Because her dad is acquainted with clinical depression, not just as a physician, but personally, he realized she might be experiencing a clinical depression, brought on by a chemical imbalance. (Those born with a chemical imbalance may not experience depression until they have their first major stress, and then the symptoms of the imbalance become recognizable.) I love it when Kathy tells women that "Prozac" is not a dirty word. She says, and I cheer, "Good for you for getting help." Depression is complicated, and often there is not just *one* simple solution. There are so many Christians who unintentionally heap shame and guilt on their depressed brothers and sisters, telling them that antidepressants are wrong, and that they should simply trust God. Would they tell a diabetic to forgo his insulin and trust God? Jesus said, "The sick need a physician," so we went to a physician.

In recent years, studies have found that people who have a chemical imbalance of some kind, leading to a clinical depression or a mental illness, and who do *not* get medical help, can suffer permanent damage to their brains. It has also been discovered that it can be detrimental to go off and on medication when there is a genuine imbalance. Each time the individual goes back on, their antidepressant is less effective. Oh, the pain we can inflict on others, when we, in our arrogance, give advice where we are uninformed.

When Sally went forward at that Christian concert, she had a heart change toward her sister. Now, with medicine for her chemical imbalance, her body began to heal as well. She was eating again, sleeping again. Sally continues:

We spent six years together before I went to college. The night before I was to leave, she climbed up on my top bunk and got under the covers with me. I was just holding her and we prayed a little together and then she looked at me. With tears in her eyes, she said, "You know what, Sally?"

I said, "What, Annie?"

"You're my very best friend."

*I said, "God, thank You. Thank You for being faithful for changing my heart
and giving me a love that I didn't have on my own. Thank You for healing me
and my relationship with my sister."*

Again, there is definitely a relationship between walking in the light and
walking in love. Even if we don't choose to walk in the light at first, He gives
us a second chance, a chance to respond to the conviction of God. John
makes it clear that we will all make bad choices—that is part of our human
nature. He writes:

If we claim to be without sin, we deceive ourselves and the truth is not in us.
(1 John 1:8)

But when we realize we've made a bad choice, then we have another
choice. We can either resist the Spirit of God, as Cain did, or we can fall on
our knees in repentance, telling Him: *I am truly sorry.*

Repentance always opens the floodgates to healing and love. That's what
happened for Sally. That's what will happen for all of us. God *will* forgive
and God *will* restore. John continues:

*If we confess our sins, he is faithful and just and will forgive us our sins and
purify us from all unrighteousness.* (1 John 1:9)

What happens when we respond to the conviction of God? The words He
spoke to Cain are very interesting. The NIV translation is "If you do what is
right, will you not be accepted?" (Genesis 4:7a). He is saying, "Is there not
forgiveness?" The Hebrew word translated "accepted" comes from a root
word meaning "to lift up." God will lift the burden from our shoulders and
the despair from our hearts. He will loosen the grip of sin from our lives. But
if we refuse to respond to the light, "sin is crouching at the door," desiring
to overpower us. And sometimes it will.

Cain refuses. He blows his second chance. So, just as God predicted, sin
overpowers him, and Cain plans and carries out the murder of his brother.

CAIN SLAYING ABEL

PETER PAUL RUBENS (1577–1640)

There is something particularly dark about hurting your *brother* or your *sister,* whether your bond is the blood of your parents or the blood of Christ. John will expound on this later, but for now, notice how often the Scripture emphasizes that this sin was done to Cain's *brother.*

> Now Cain said to his **brother** Abel, "Let's go out to the field."
> And while they were in the field, Cain attacked his **brother** Abel and killed him.
> Then the LORD said to Cain, "Where is your **brother** Abel?"
> "I don't know," he replied. "Am I my **brother's** keeper?"
> The LORD said, "What have you done? Listen! Your **brother's** blood cries out to
> me from the ground." (Genesis 4:8–10)

CHANCE # 3: REPENT OF YOUR SIN

The amazing truth is that if you read the above account of Genesis 4:8–10 carefully, even after Cain had murdered his brother, God was offering yet again an opportunity for forgiveness. The Lord amazes us that way. Why did God ask, "Where is your brother Abel?" Of course God *knew* Cain had murdered Abel. But He wanted Cain to confess the truth to Him and to repent of his sin.

(Kathy) This is why I give women the opportunity to come forward for prayer at the end of most of my events. I believe great power is unleashed in you through repentance. Whether you get up out of your seat or confess your sin to a trusted friend, the act of true repentance solidifies the fact that you mean business with God. It shows Him that you want all He has, acknowledging a desperate need for the love and mercy that only He can give. It's easy to hide in the dark. It's much harder to step into the light. John told us that would be our natural response, "to love the dark," because our deeds are evil. But when you make the choice to step into the light, no matter how hard it is, the power of God's Spirit is unleashed in your life. He then has free rein to accomplish all He desires for you.

God surely hates the shedding of innocent blood. There is no doubt about it. But He still would have forgiven Cain if Cain had confessed and repented.

We have found that one of the hardest things for women to believe is that God can forgive abortion. We've seen many women lock themselves in self-imposed prisons of guilt when God longs to forgive them. They know they have shed innocent blood. They carry its stain on their hands and the burden on their hearts. Just as when God asked Cain a question so that He could get to the truth, God longs for women to be set free from the chains they've held themselves in by acknowledging the truth.

Women might say to God, "What about my baby? What about what I did?"

And God says, "What about your baby? I have your baby. I want a relationship with you."

He never condemns us, but gives us a chance to confess, repent, and be set free of shame and guilt. He always wants to get to the truth, because the truth will set us free. Then He will fully forgive, fully cleanse.

Because so many women who have had abortions cannot believe in a love so great, in a grace so far-reaching, they carry their burden of guilt, and it affects not only them, but also their attitude toward their husbands, toward their children, and toward their world. We have seen the power of God released in women who finally can trust in His forgiveness.

(Kathy) I experienced this when I was in Turkey doing a conference for military wives. I had already sung for about an hour and a half, and the women asked me to sing some more. Because they were in no hurry to leave, I decided to sing "A Baby's Prayer." Statistics tell us that one out of every four women have had an abortion. I knew there had to be some of them there. So I said,

> "Some of you have suffered a great deal with guilt and shame from the choice of abortion. This song is for you."

Many women cried that night, confessing abortions and other sins. The prison doors were being flung open and they were being set free. The next morning, as I was preparing to sing a couple of songs, a woman came up to me and grabbed my hand. She spoke to me through teary eyes:

> "Kathy, I had an abortion twenty-five years ago. I've never told a soul. I want you to know that I slept through the night last night for the first time in twenty-five years. I feel free. I feel at peace. Thank you for allowing me to experience God's forgiveness."

What we fail to realize is that God is on our side. Remember God's heart. He is the father in the story of the Prodigal Son, the Father who opens His arms to His erring child, the Father who is willing to embrace the shame of a rebellious child, and who rejoices at His child's homecoming.

(Dee) For so many years I have wandered through art museums with my art enthusiast husband and daughter, Sally. I have been the impatient one, wondering how they can stand *so* long in front of *one* painting. But a book titled *The Return of the Prodigal* by Henri Nouwen is changing me, slowing me down, helping me see. Nouwen reminisces about the first time he saw this painting, as a poster:

> *I could not take my eyes away. I felt drawn by the intimacy between the two figures, the warm red of the man's cloak, the golden yellow of the boy's tunic, and*

THE RETURN OF THE
PRODIGAL SON

REMBRANDT (1606–1669)

the mysterious light engulfing them both. But most of all it was the hands—the old man's hands—as they touched the boy's shoulders that reached me in a place where I had never been reached before.[4]

How eager Nouwen was to go to St. Petersburg and see the original. Bigger than life it did not disappoint him. The first day he spent the whole afternoon in front of the masterpiece, making the museum guard a bit uneasy. He pulled up a chair. He took copious notes, observing each figure in the painting and how each related to the other—the colors, the light, the hands, the expressions. He observed the painting from different angles, watching how the light fell at noon, at midafternoon, and as evening approached. Nouwen's time with Rembrandt's masterpiece deepened his walk with God like nothing else had ever done. To give you just a glimpse through Nouwen's eyes, consider one truth he discovered: Rembrandt had portrayed not only the strength of a father's love toward his erring children, but also the tenderness of a mother:

The father's left hand touching the shoulder is strong and muscular. The fingers are spread out and cover a large part of the prodigal son's shoulder and back. I can see a certain pressure, especially in the thumb. That hand seems not only to touch, but also, with its strength, to hold . . .

How different is the father's right hand! This hand does not hold or grasp. It is refined, soft, and very tender. The fingers are close to each other and have an elegant quality. It lies gently upon the son's shoulder. It wants to caress, to stroke, and to offer consolation and comfort. It is a mother's hand. [5]

Nouwen also began to see the wing-like qualities in the father's cape, reminding him of the words of Jesus when He cried:

O Jerusalem, Jerusalem, you who kill the prophets and stone those sent to you, how often I have longed to gather your children together, as a hen gathers her chicks under her wings, but you were not willing. (Matthew 23:37)

There is so much more to this masterpiece. In many ways, Rembrandt portrayed the central truth of the parable of Jesus: God will *always* open His arms and welcome us home.

(Kathy) I often tell women:

You can't "out-sin" the love of God. He's not going to appear to you one day and say, "I've had it. You really did it this time. That's it. I'm done." If that were true, His dying on the cross would all be in vain. Because we calculate things and see things through the eyes of our human nature, we think there is going to be an end to His love.

We think that the Forgiveness River is going to run dry because we've dipped in it one too many times. I know, I've been there, but He says, "It will never happen." Please, don't ever give up on God and how much He loves you. And don't give up on yourself—because that is when death will have free rein in you. That is when the enemy will have a heyday. He wants to win.

Until you close your eyes for that last time on earth, there is always hope. So always take the opportunity to say, "Lord, I give this to You once again."

It's like the thief on the cross. When he humbled himself and acknowledged the Savior of the World, God said to him, "Today you will be with Me in Paradise." Yes, today God hears you, wherever you've been, whatever you've done. He'll say,

"Take my hand. We're going to conquer this thing together."

THE RADIANT COLORS OF HOPE

If you allow God's light into your life, if you choose the light, if you respond to the light, you'll find a new sense of hope springing up in your soul. If you continue to do "the next right thing" when you wake up in the morning, if that is your goal for the day, it begins to add up. The days become weeks. The weeks become months. The months become years. Before you know it, you're operating in a different place. Your patterns are changed. Where you used to do something, you don't do it anymore. Where you used to feel something, you are quick to give it over to God, knowing that feelings come and go. This is when you can live in the joy of your freedom. This is the joy and the victory that we have experienced in so many areas of our lives: in Kathy's battle with bulimia; in her relationship with her mother; and in her ability to forgive those who had slandered her; in Dee's marriage; and in her daughter Sally and her response to her little sister. Whatever it is—and each of us has that "thing" that seems impossible to be delivered from—God is on your side. He loves you, and He longs to transform you into His beautiful bride.

Recently Kathy had an experience in which God showed her, again, His heart for His Bride—how He loves us and longs for us to respond in true repentance to Him. We *knew* this intellectually, but He made it real in a new, powerful, and unforgettable way.

If we walk in the light, as he is in the light, we have fellowship with one another, and the blood of Jesus, his Son, purifies us from all sin.

CHAPTER 5

WALKING IN THE LIGHT

(Kathy)

I have been adding "Evenings for Women" to my calendar. They are special nights when I sing and speak to women of all ages. I have been in awe of the Lord as He has wooed women down to the altar for healing in their hearts—for renewal, restoration, and revival. Miraculous healing has washed over the souls of these women, and I have watched in amazement. As the night draws to a close, I can see it on their faces. They leave with new hope.

In the days that follow the events, I often ponder what has gone on. I find myself greatly delighted at what God is doing, and I often pray that the women won't lose the release and the freedom they felt when they were on their knees. Once, when I was praying over a woman, a picture came into my mind. As I placed my hands on top of her head, I saw streams of oil pouring over her whole body. That beautiful picture stayed with me.

In the days following, I began to envision myself anointing the women with oil as I prayed over them. This picture included me drawing a sign of the cross on their foreheads. I really wasn't sure what it all meant. I hadn't researched it. I let this vision play in my mind for quite a while. I never want to do anything, especially involving the Beloved of God, if I don't have a true conviction in my gut that I should.

It used to be that times of prayer at my concerts were few and far between. But as I have been stepping out and speaking, as well as singing, and doing so many women's events, the whole face of what I do has changed. I welcome it wholeheartedly. Women are responding, pouring down to the front, sometimes even before I give an invitation. Because of this, we are now asking for intercessors in that particular city to be prepared to pray for other women if the need arises.

Our Mysterious God

A thrilling experience happened at one of these evenings in Grand Rapids. I walked into a room in the church where six or seven intercessors were waiting to greet me. I explained what to expect from the evening, as best I could, as I've learned God may do the unexpected if we are willing to let go of our own agendas. Then I prayed with them. As I got up to leave, one of the women said,

"Kathy, can we pray over you?"
"Absolutely," I said eagerly.

I got on my knees as the women gathered around me. All of a sudden about three women pulled out little vials of oil. I know this is probably not uncommon if you have been brought up in certain denominations, but I've been prayed over by many believers in many churches, and in twenty years, less than a handful have ever pulled out vials of oil. One woman moved toward me and anointed me on my forehead as she made the sign of the cross. I was overwhelmed by this intimate touch of God. But in the glory of this moment, a sudden thought occurred to me:

Lord . . . You're not trying to tell me something here—are You? I mean, this is just for me—isn't it? . . . Surely You don't want me to do this tonight—do You? For all these women? And besides, Lord, suppose someone has a problem with me doing this? Are You really telling me to do this?

The Lord was immediate in His response. "Yes, I am."

We finished praying and I tried to quickly explain. I told the women the picture that had been coming to me in the last few months: the anointing of oil, the sign of the cross, the picture of a woman being bathed in the healing of God. Then I told them what had just happened as they had been praying for me. I said to the ladies,

"I sense God is telling me to do this tonight, so help me quickly understand. I don't ever want to do things on the platform that I'm not quite sure about or are confusing to the women. Do you have some nuggets of truth I can remember when the time comes?"

One woman gently said, with strength and conviction, "Kathy, just remember it is the power, purpose, and presence of God. You are praying and bestowing the power, purpose, presence of God on that person."

I said, "Okay, okay—power, purpose, presence. Power, purpose, presence. Got it."

As I stepped onto the stage that night, I saw one of the vials by my books on the podium. It warmed my heart. I couldn't wait to see what God would do.

At the close of the evening, I sat at the edge of the stage and spoke as honestly as I could with the women.

Many of you have come here tonight with lots of baggage. I'm sure we can all relate to that overwhelming weight on our souls. We want freedom. We want to be released. The Lord always offers hope. The Lord always has an outstretched hand. He not only longs to give you a new day, but a new way of going through your trials and sorrows.

I believe God wants me to anoint some of you with oil. You must know this is all new to me. But this is what I felt like the Lord told me to do tonight. Let me explain how I feel it will help you . . .

As you abandon yourself in prayer you will be opening yourself up to His purposes for your life. He will bestow upon you His power, and He will grant you the

manifestation of His presence. I don't know how many of you would like to do this,
but I'm willing to stay here as long as I need to for the Lord to meet you.

And ladies, remember, as ridiculous as this sounds, we must realize this is not
some hocus-pocus magic potion that will poof you into freedom. This is sacred.

As women were coming for prayer I saw that there were four lines form-
ing, going all the way down the aisles of the church. For four hours I
anointed women. The sign of the cross was placed on a thousand foreheads.
I will never forget how sacred the atmosphere was. Women looked at me
through tears and whispered, tenderly, "Thank you, Kathy."

I sensed all night God was saying to these women:

You are loved.
I hear you.
I will carry that burden.

(Dee) The experience Kathy had fascinated me, because I have been so
aware of the call of God to His Bride to have greater faith, to live purer lives,
to "rely" as John tells us, "on the love God has for us" (1 John 4:16), and to
abandon ourselves to Him. He doesn't want us to be content with salvation,
He wants us to be holy so that we can be arrayed with the colors of His love.
When Kathy told me about anointing the women, I pondered it and considered what it meant. What is God saying to us? And what about anointing
with oil? Is it appropriate today?

Anointing for Ministry

There is a great deal of mystery associated with the ritual, but it is helpful to
see how it was used in the Scriptures. In the Old Testament, priests and
future kings were anointed. It represented sanctification, the setting apart of
an individual, as a priest or a king, and the wonderful extravagant grace of
the Lord. The Scriptures say that the oil that anointed Aaron, consecrating
him as a priest, flowed down his head, to his beard, and to the collar of his

robe. It was precious and indicative of great blessing from God. *But it is also interesting that anointing someone did not assure godliness on the part of that individual.* There must be a response of living, day by day, in true repentance. In Exodus 30, Aaron is being anointed with oil. But by Exodus 32, Aaron is allowing the people, who were impatient waiting for Moses to come down from the mountain, to build and worship a gold calf!

THE WORSHIP OF
THE GOLDEN CALF

NICOLAS POUSSIN (1594–1665)

We see the same thing with King Saul and King David. God's Spirit, as represented by the oil, could be quenched. Saul and David were both anointed with oil, but they led very different lives. Saul walked primarily in the dark, living a disobedient life, whereas David was a man after God's heart, and walked in the light. When David sinned, he truly repented, turning back to the light.

When Kathy and I were in Atlanta, speaking to women in ministry, we felt strongly led to anoint them with oil. One of the characteristics of truth, according to John's letter, is that God's Spirit and God's Word never conflict. God will not lead you, for example, to commit adultery. So when you think God is leading you to do something unusual, you should always ask, "Does this conflict with His Word?" So before I was going to go along with my wild friend Kathy (who is *usually* right, but also tends to be impulsive), I asked God, "Please, show me in Your Word if this is appropriate."

I knew that anointing of priests was appropriate in the Old Testament. Suddenly, I realized, under the New Covenant, *every* believer is a priest! That was the confirmation from the Word that I needed.

After Jesus became our High Priest, He called *every* believer to be a priest under His authority, ministering to others (1 Peter 2:9). Jesus came "to preach good news . . . to bind up the brokenhearted, to proclaim freedom for the captives" (Isaiah 61:1). Now we, who follow in His steps, bring this message as well. Later, I also thought, that though a believer may not be *literally* anointed with oil, we absolutely *must* be anointed by the Spirit, or our ministry will be of no avail. We *must* live out the principles of John, the principles of light, death, truth, and mercy, and then the oil will run down, flowing into the lives of those around us. Charles Spurgeon writes:

> *Every Christian is a priest, but he cannot execute the priestly office without unction, and hence we must go day by day to God the Holy Ghost, that we may have our heads anointed with oil.*

ANOINTING FOR WELCOMING AND HEALING

Anointing was used for other reasons in the Scriptures. It was sometimes used as a sign of welcome, protection, or healing. Those who are sick are told to call upon the elders, meaning those in leadership in the body, to pray over them and anoint them with oil. The word *sick* can refer to both emotional and physical burdens.

> *Is any one of you sick? He should call the elders of the church to pray over him and anoint him with oil in the name of the Lord.* (James 5:14)

But notice, again, the oil is not some magic potion; the individual must respond. See what James says next:

> *And the prayer offered in faith will make the sick person well; the Lord will raise him up. If he has sinned, he will be forgiven. Therefore confess your sins to*

each other and pray for each other so that you may be healed. The prayer of a right-eous man is powerful and effective. (James 5:15–16)

Some denominations are more comfortable anointing believers with oil than are others. Some do it only for those *physically* ill, and only by men in the *office* of elders. Some do it for those who have emotional hurts as well, and the anointing is done by anyone who is considered to be a mature leader. But I think we can all agree that it is a sacred act and must be approached in the fear of God. It *is* associated with God's blessing and faithfulness, but there is also a call, on the part of the individual, to faith and obedience.

We believe that God pours out His Spirit upon His sons and daughters, and that He is reminding us of who we are in Christ. This is what John is saying in his letter:

How great is the love the Father has lavished on us, that we should be called children of God! And that is what we are! The reason the world does not know us is that it did not know him. (1 John 3:1)

But even though God has lavished His love on us, even though we are His children, His betrothed, we must act like it. We *must* be responsive and responsible. We must be constantly aware that we carry the reputation of Christ.

We are in the time of separation, but our Bridegroom is coming back, perhaps very soon, and we need to be ready. In Atlanta, when Kathy and I anointed women in ministry with oil we found ourselves whispering: "You are His Bride" or "You are His Beloved." It was such a sweet reminder of what John told believers in his letter.

REMEMBER WHO YOU ARE

John's letter is full of tender reassurances, but also a call to be holy. In 1 John 2:12–14, he pauses and addresses believers in various levels of maturity—from those who have just come into relationship with God to those who have known the Lord for a long time. John knows that he will soon leave this world, that time is running out, and he is saying the most important things to these precious believers. He was not only praying and writing for that generation, but for us. Picture John among you, taking your face in his hands, looking in your eyes, and gently saying:

> *Dear child, your sins have been forgiven.*
> *Dear woman, you know Him who has been from the beginning.*
> *Young girl, you have overcome the evil one.*
> *Dear beloved, the Word of God lives in you.* (Based on 1 John 2:12–14)

Throughout his letter, John is continually reminding us of who we are in Christ, of the power available to us. The Lord longs for His Bride to trust Him enough to abandon herself to Him. He longs for her to be ready for His return, for her "wedding gown" to be clean and bright, and arrayed with the colors of His love.

WHY WE MUST BE HOLY

(Kathy) Recently when Dee and I were in Lexington, Kentucky, I was greeting women at my merchandise table. I've often said that I love this time of sharing. I often talk about the "connection" with the women: their stories, their prayers, and their gifts. As I signed CD covers, shook hands, and even hugged some of the women, I was thanking the Lord for these tender souls before me. I kept smiling, but all the while I was gripped by the Presence of God:

> *Kath, what you're doing, where I have you, what you see here right now—it's about them. It's all about My love for them.*

As I reflected on that moment afterward, I knew what the Lord was trying to say to me. I must never take these opportunities He is giving me for granted. I know there must be a surrendering on my part that allows the Lord to represent Himself as He would desire to represent Himself to His Bride. Can God reach His people any way He chooses? Of course! He used a donkey. But God was clearly calling me to greater holiness and a deeper love. I *must* be the woman these people think I am. I can't just come home from my conference after I've laid my hands on women to be healed from breast cancer, or to be free from addictions or abuse, and then just live my life as if I took part in a play. I can't just say:

> *Okay, that was the "minister Kathy Troccoli" on Friday night or Saturday afternoon. But now I can be the "everyday Kathy Troccoli" and coast Monday through Thursday on a sea of apathy and mediocrity.*

Let's never forget: Anything we say or anything we boldly declare, we must be striving to live out. Private? Public? Is there a person for each? The representation of Christ should be the same in both places.

(Dee) As I listen to Kathy, I understand, for I am faced with a similar responsibility. Scripture is clear that teachers and ministers of the Word will be judged more severely. There have been times when I am writing a Bible study guide and the fear of God washes over me. I could almost tremble. Once, when Steve and I were writing a guide and we were truly struggling with a particular topic, I went to sleep with this thought in my head: *O Lord, You are pretty blatant about some things in Your Word. Some of it is extremely black and white—there seems to be no room for any gray.* Before I went to sleep I struggled with how I was going to present this topic. My last thought before I closed my eyes was: *Perhaps tomorrow I can find a way to soften what seems so severe.*

In the middle of the night, I was awakened by a Holy Presence, and I sat straight up in bed.

> *Do not tamper with my Word.*

The next morning I wrote the lesson. I didn't add to the Word. I didn't "soften" the Word. Did the lesson seem severe? Absolutely. But truth without love is judgment and love without truth is destructive.

We always have to ask ourselves when we struggle with the severity of God's Word:

> *Do we think we "get it" more?*

Do we think we have more mercy than God does?
Do we think we have greater rationale and wisdom than the Almighty One?

We forget that we are dealing with the God of the universe. As the Lord questioned Job, He could question us:

Were you there when I laid the earth's foundation?
Have you ever given orders to the morning?
Can you bring forth the constellations in their seasons?
Do you send the lightning bolts on their way?
Can you tip over the water jars of the heavens?
(Based on Job 38:4a, 12a, 32a, 35a, 37b)

The Lord also says:

Who is this that darkens my counsel with words without knowledge? . . .
Will the one who contends with the Almighty correct him? (Job 38:2; 40:2a)

Get the picture? We've all been there. We're not saying it's wrong to wrestle with God or question Him. It is vital that you dig into the Word, especially those passages that are shrouded in mystery, and ask God, "What does this *really* mean?" Yet there are also times when our Bridegroom simply is not making sense, and we cry out, "Why are You allowing this pain in my life or my loved one's life?" That's not wrong either. In fact, in the Old Testament, the Lord encourages it, saying, "Come now, let us reason together" (Isaiah 1:18a). But so often we contend with Him as if He is our next-door neighbor, or debate with Him as if He's some professor at a university. One of the hardest things for believers, and even more ridiculous to the world, is that often God's answer is simply:

Because I am God.

BE HOLY, AS I AM HOLY

When we stated that teachers and ministers of the Word will be judged more severely, it is not because God holds such people in any higher regard. It's because if such leaders twist the Word, they'll twist the road on which many are traveling to get closer to God. So we will be judged more severely.

Does this mean that if you don't sing or speak or write books that you are exempt from living a life that is holy? Absolutely not. Whether you are a nurse, a mother, a lawyer, a hair stylist, or an administrator, you will always be affecting those around you. Each soul is precious to God. Some of the most severe warnings of Jesus are directed toward those who lead "little ones" astray. What an enormous responsibility we each have. Because each of us affects those around us for good or for evil, we are all called to be pure, all called to be holy. Peter writes:

> As obedient children, do not conform to the evil desires you had when you lived in ignorance. But just as he who called you is holy, so be holy in all you do; for it is written: "Be holy, because I am holy." (1 Peter 1:14–16)

We must be vigilant to seek the godly path in all we do. We will never become loving and holy women of God unless we are continually willing to get out of the way and let God have His way.

Peter talked about "when we lived in ignorance." It's funny that this statement came from the apostle Peter because it is clear he made so many ignorant choices. Peter was impulsive and often jumped to the wrong conclusions. He had the audacity to tell Jesus not to go to the cross. Peter also willfully sinned, even denying his Lord. But Jesus loved Peter. He continually called Peter to holiness. What transformed Peter into a wise, holy, and mighty man of God? Repentance.

LIVING IN A STATE OF CONTINUAL REPENTANCE

The only way we can walk in the light is to live in a state of continual repentance. It is the cornerstone of the Christian faith. As many times as we have read the story of Jesus washing the feet of the disciples, it was Pastor Erwin Lutzer of Moody Memorial Church who helped us, through a radio broadcast, to see the symbolism. As you read this familiar story that John tells, see if you can visualize how it symbolizes the teachings of "walking in the light":

> He came to Simon Peter, who said to him, "Lord, are you going to wash my feet?"
>
> Jesus replied, "You do not realize now what I am doing, but later you will understand."
>
> "No," said Peter, "you shall never wash my feet."
>
> Jesus answered, "Unless I wash you, you have no part with me."
>
> "Then, Lord," Simon Peter replied, "not just my feet but my hands and my head as well!" (John 13:6–9)

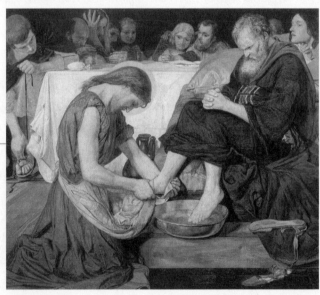

CHRIST WASHING
PETER'S FEET

FORD MADOX BROWN
(1821–1893)

"UNLESS I WASH YOU, YOU HAVE NO PART WITH ME"

Own feet carry us into all kinds of dark places. Notice the beautiful symbolism here. How often must we be washed? In the days of Jesus, people needed to have their feet washed daily, or several times a day. On a symbolic level, that is true of us as well. Every day we are not only contending with the evil of our own hearts, but we are surrounded by the pollution of the mass media and the world. We get dirty. That's why we must cry out to God, just as Peter did:

Not just my feet but my hands and my head as well!

(*Kathy*) When a Christian is filled with grumbling, hate, and judgmental comments toward others, I often think, *What do they do when the door is closed and they talk to Jesus? Are they aware of their capacity to sin? Are they aware of the darkness in their hearts?* If you really talk to God about your behavior, I don't think you can have that kind of an attitude toward someone—at least not for long. You will always be convicted to show mercy, no matter someone's sin, if you are honest with God about yourself. If you stay in a state of continual repentance for your own sins, judgmentalism will not rule over you. Repentance allows God's light to reveal your pride. He will show you your sin. Then the mercy you receive from the Lord for yourself can be given to others. When I find myself getting judgmental, I usually tell myself:

Troccoli, you need a spiritual shower.

True repentance will make us holier and will help us to show more Christlike love to others. But it must be a true repentance.

Although I wasn't brought up in the evangelical church, I had many friends who joked with me, saying that every other Sunday, or every youth retreat, they would go to the altar to "get saved." In a more serious way, I hear the frustration of many women:

"I've confessed this a thousand times."

"I thought I laid this down."

"How can God take me seriously?"

It is very possible that what they have experienced is not genuine repentance, but the counterfeit. Just as Satan counterfeits everything else, he counterfeits repentance. It is important that we look at a few forms of counterfeit repentance.

COUNTERFEIT # 1: EMOTIONAL REPENTANCE WITHOUT A U-TURN

(Dee) One of my favorite people is Bible teacher Jan Silvious. She is *so* real, down-to-earth, and wise. When she counsels people who call into her radio broadcast, she cuts right to the heart of the problem, like an expert surgeon. She has helped thousands of women to "get well." My husband describes her counsel as a triple dose of common sense.

Jan is continually urging all of us to be "big girl Christians" instead of "little girl Christians." Once, when I was speaking with Jan at a women's event, there was an altar call, and many women came forward. Some stayed up there a long time, sobbing. Afterward, Jan and I took a walk outside. It was a balmy summer night in the Smoky Mountains, and as we walked along the quaint little streets of Gatlinburg, I was eager to hear her thoughts about all that had transpired that night. She told me about a friend who asked her once, "What's your favorite bad feeling?"

Then Jan said, "Ever since that time I have learned to ask that question when I see emotional responses."

I realized that what Jan was saying was that many of us, particularly as women, like to *feel* things and hold on to them. Somehow it makes us feel more alive. Of course emotion in itself is not bad, it's just that we can "camp around feelings" that cause destruction. We can settle into self-pity, anger, guilt, and all sorts of webs. That's why, especially as women, we may weep before God but do nothing about our self-made prisons. They have become comfortable for us.

Right now our youngest child, Annie, who is nineteen, is with Youth with a Mission. During Thanksgiving break, she told me:

> *Mom, I used to go to the altar weeping, but then I didn't do anything about it. Now I am going to the altar and not weeping, and doing something about it.*

Jan Silvious has experienced the frustration, as a counselor, of seeing the tears but no behavioral change. She has heard, as I have, people plead with God, saying:

I only want Your will, Lord.

Let me be the woman You want me to be.

Why aren't You hearing my prayers?

The problem is that those are empty prayers when one doesn't obey even the simple things that God has *already* revealed to them.

A passage in Malachi shows men weeping and wailing at the altar, but they do not see that their repentance is counterfeit. They have dealt treacherously with their wives, casting them aside, neglecting their marriage vows. Their hearts are so hard they do not even have the mercy to give their abandoned wives certificates of divorce, setting them free. (In those days, since these women had not been set free to remarry, they were destitute, as women without a man had no means of support.) The great irony in this passage is that now these heartless men are miffed at God for not responding to their prayers. God clearly tells them their sin:

> *. . . the LORD is acting as the witness between you and the wife of your youth, because you have broken faith with her, though she is your partner, the wife of your marriage covenant.* (Malachi 2:14)

So often the phrase "I hate divorce" is taken out of context from this passage in Malachi, and though it is true that God *does* hate divorce, what He is saying here is that He hates the treachery that leads a man (or a woman) to abandon his spouse. God has a heart of mercy toward the victim. God *does* release the spouse who has been abandoned. The phrase in 1 Corinthians, "not bound," is the strongest possible word for freedom. If the unbeliever wants to go, God says, "Let him do so. A believing man or woman is not bound in such circumstances" (1 Corinthians 7:15). He or she is set free to remarry. That is the mercy of God toward the victim.

Does this mean God does not have mercy toward the one who did the treachery? God will always forgive, though there may still be consequences. He would have forgiven the men of Malachi's day had they *truly* repented. You can't fool God with lots of tears. He sees straight into the heart. How their false repentance angers God:

Another thing you do: You flood the LORD's altar with tears. You weep and wail because he no longer pays attention to your offerings or accepts them with pleasure from your hands. (Malachi 2:13)

God wants *true* repentance, a holy fear of Him, a complete U-turn—gut-wrenching emotion and a cover-up of the sin are only going to make Him angrier.

There is another counterfeit that looks real, because there is an actual behavioral change. Yet even that can be a counterfeit.

COUNTERFEIT # 2: SORRY ABOUT CONSEQUENCES BUT NOT BROKEN BEFORE GOD

It is possible to change your behavior because you are sorry for the consequences, but unless your heart is broken before God, you will not experience His power. Soon your own strength gives out and you revert to your old behavior. King Saul, for example, was envious of David and tried to murder him. Saul's son, Jonathan, went to his father and said:

Why then would you do wrong to an innocent man like David by killing him for no reason? (1 Samuel 19:5c)

SAUL LISTENING
TO DAVID PLAYING
THE HARP
_____
ERASMUS QUELLINUS (C.1650)

Saul *seems* repentant and surely has the right words and, for a little while, the right behavior:

> Saul listened to Jonathan and took this oath: "As surely as the LORD lives, David will not be put to death."
>
> So Jonathan called David and told him the whole conversation. He brought him to Saul, and David was with Saul as before. (1 Samuel 19:6–7)

Quellinus shows Saul with David, as David plays his harp. But notice Saul's countenance, his body language, and his grip on his spear. This is not a man broken before God. This is a man who has repented outwardly because he regrets the consequences of estrangement with his son, but his heart is not broken before God. It doesn't take long for his strength to give out, and soon he is again throwing spears at David.

We can engage in alcohol abuse, sexual immorality, and other costly behavior, and be sorry for the consequences. We see the toll it takes on our body. We see the devastation it can cause family and friends. Because we want to save our own skin, we turn for a time, *but unless we are repentant toward God, our own strength will always give out.* There's no true turning away from the sin and so no true power from the Holy Spirit for lasting change.

King David, in contrast, was truly broken before God when confronted with his sin of sexual immorality and murder. In the famous penitential Psalm 51, he says:

> Against you, you only, have I sinned and done what is evil in your sight. (Psalm 51:4)

That phrase has confused some, for surely David sinned against others when he committed adultery and murder. What godly men and women have come to see in this verse is that it isn't that David doesn't realize his sin toward man, but that God now looms above him as so awesome and holy that he can see no one else. He must first get right with God, the ultimate authority over his life. In *My Utmost for His Highest,* Oswald Chambers writes:

> Very few of us know anything about conviction of sin. We know the experience of being disturbed because we have done wrong things. But conviction of sin by the

Holy Spirit blots out every relationship on earth and makes us aware of only one—
"Against You, You only, have I sinned."[1]

Does this mean we have to be brokenhearted every time we fail in our daily lives—every time we are irritable with someone, or rude, or forgetful of someone's needs? Though you will not always have the same sense of grief, you should always be aware that you have indeed grieved or offended God by hurting someone else. Your repentance, to be true, must be toward Him, as well as the one you have hurt.

COUNTERFEIT # 3: A PARTIAL TURN INSTEAD OF A U-TURN

When you are truly sorry toward God, you are willing to give up the sin He shows you and to do whatever He tells you to do to make things right. Again, Saul exemplifies the counterfeit. When God told him to wipe out *all* of the Amalekites, Saul obeyed partially, keeping the king and the best of the livestock alive.

We have such deceitful hearts. We often resort to our own rational. This results in partial obedience. We repent of some of what God has convicted us of, but if we don't feel quite that convicted about it, we may hold on to the sin, so that we can have access to it when we desire it. We avoid the full U-turn because we rationalize that we aren't in full-fledged sin. We want partial credit for partial repentance. We will always come out looking good if we compare ourselves to Jack the Ripper, but if we compare ourselves to Jesus Christ, we will hang our heads low. When Saul had *partially* obeyed God, he greeted Samuel with:

> *The LORD bless you! I have carried out the LORD's instructions.* (1 Samuel 15:13)

But Samuel said,

> *What then is this bleating of sheep in my ears? What is this lowing of cattle that I hear?* (1 Samuel 15:14)

Samuel also tells Saul:

SAUL AND THE
WITCH OF ENDOR

BENJAMIN WEST (1738–1820)

*You have rejected the word of the LORD, and the LORD has rejected you as king
over Israel!* (1 Samuel 15:26b)

This wasn't enough to cause Saul to make a U-turn. He continued his life
of disobedience. When facing a battle against the Philistines, near the close
of his life, instead of going to the Lord for wisdom, he secretly goes to the
witch of Endor. At his request, she calls up Samuel from the dead, who gives
him dreaded news: the Lord is going to hand him over to the Philistines.

Saul certainly exemplified counterfeit repentance. He deceived himself.
The word *repentance* means "change": a change of heart toward God, and a
change of behavior. At the altar, remorse and repentance *look* the same.
Remorse is being sorry for the consequences, but not a conviction that we
have grieved God. Remorse is sorry for the pain, but is not willing to give
up, long term, whatever is causing the pain. Remorse may give up part of the
sin, but it holds on to the sin, unwilling to take a true U-turn.

(Kathy) When you really think about it, why aren't we grieved about our
sin before God? I think it is hardness of heart. Perhaps we've let anger and
disillusionment reign. There's the woman who is angry with God over the
loss of her baby, or her marriage, or her health—she lets all that get in the
way. You aren't going to be repentant before a God with whom you are
angry. Perhaps we've let apathy reign—there's the woman who has taken her

love relationship with Jesus for granted and allowed the things of this world to steal her affections. If we are not intimate with God, we are not going to respond with repentance when we've hurt Him. When we hurt an acquaintance, the weight of the "I'm sorry" is going to be weaker than when we hurt a dear friend. If we are casual with God our repentance will be just as casual.

Years ago when I was at my counselor's office, she was requesting that I respond in certain ways with which I didn't agree. We went back and forth as I tried to defend myself. She finally said, "Listen, Kathy. Who has the better track record? You or me? If you don't want my help, stay home."

Boy, did that rattle me. I took her words to heart. Sometimes we *say* we want certain things, but we aren't willing to make a change. We hold fast to our old ways of living and communicating—we don't really hand them over to God and allow Him to change us. I've had women pour their hearts out to me about a particular situation they've been dealing with, and the friend or sister that they're with will roll her eyes. I can see from that response that their sad song has played like a broken record. They want me to give them a new answer or a new revelation, yet what they really need to do is make a U-turn.

TRUE REPENTANCE AND PURIFICATION

In discussing repentance, author Henry Brandt told of driving to Chicago with his wife. Somewhere along the way he made a wrong turn, but he didn't want to admit it. They kept seeing signs that gave the miles to Detroit, and his wife thought that odd, but Brandt was reluctant to admit he had taken a wrong road. He kept trying to figure out a way to turn around without actually turning around. True repentance always involves admitting we are wrong *and* humbling ourselves before God *and* making a full U-turn away from the sin. We simply *cannot* get back on the right track without a broken heart before God and a complete U-turn.

We are in the process of being transformed, and we struggle every day with sin. But we can experience real victory when God purifies us.

Look again at 1 John 1:7, and see if you can discern the two things that will follow true repentance:

If we walk in the light, as he is in the light, we have fellowship with one another, and the blood of Jesus, his Son, purifies us from all sin.

Do you see? We will love one another and we will be purified. How He longs for us to be pure, so that His river of life will flow out purely to others: refreshing, cleansing, and restoring them. When we are not clean, when we are murky and polluted, the water that flows out discourages, depresses, and defeats those around us. Our relationships, instead of being sweet, become sour. Instead of harmonious, they are discordant. Instead of uplifting, they are discouraging. If relationships in your life look this way, it is a warning bell that there may be persistent pollution in your river.

Kathy's friend Allyson talks about our "sin structure." That vivid term speaks about the sin that so easily besets us: whether it is a critical spirit, a bad temper, a lying or a gossiping tongue—whatever—it keeps rearing its ugly head, for it seems to be so deeply rooted in our very being. Many of these sins may have been learned from parents, and we will pass them on to our children unless we allow the Spirit of God to cleanse them from us and teach us a new way to respond. We can't camp out and say, "That's just the way I am."

It doesn't matter who we are, or where we've been, or the kind of household in which we've been brought up. What matters is who He is in us. If there is a characteristic in a believer that is not Christlike, it must change. And it can change. Can you imagine conversing with Jesus and Him saying:

"I really don't want you to get as angry as you do."

Only a fool would respond: "That's just the way I am."

Listen to what God has spoken into our darkness.

I really don't want you to put up that wall.
Don't close down so fast.
You resort so quickly to self-pity.
You never say you're sorry.

This whole book could be filled with the things the Lord speaks to us about our character. He yearns for us to become like Him and has even provided supernatural ways that we can, but we still dig our heels into the mud of arrogance, ignorance, and unbelief and say, "That's just the way I am."

(Dee) I've wallowed from time to time in the mud myself. I have a critical spirit. I always see the thing that is wrong. I have often written about our daughter Beth, whom we adopted from an orphanage in Thailand. I had a tremendous struggle with the habits she developed in her most formative years. She had never been taught any of the simple customs of graciousness. She was continually burping, spitting, and showing a general lack of manners.

Though I wanted to be a loving mother to Beth, I had trouble "staying in the light." I was more like the car that is speeding down a dark country road lit by occasional lampposts. Now and then the light would flash into my window, but darkness prevailed.

My state of heart deeply affected my relationship with my daughter. She didn't particularly want to be with me. I *did* encourage Beth, but it was not the pattern of my life. A few years after we adopted her, I pleaded with the Lord. I knew my relationship could be much richer with my daughter. I asked Him to show me His will and His purpose for me as Beth's mother. As always He began to reveal to me His wisdom and gave me eyes to see Beth as He did. She was in desperate need of many things. For her first twelve years, she had been deprived of affirmation. When Steve and I went to pick her up in Bangkok, all she possessed was in a shoebox. Her cup was absolutely empty.

Many times we don't give any heed to people's past. We process our feelings for them by what we see in the present moment. The things that bothered me about Beth were things she couldn't possibly have prevented. *What was I thinking—being annoyed by them?* My critical nature glared at me. Its ugliness made me realize I was not only grieving Beth, but also the heart of God.

I was determined to change. I moved farther into the light by encouraging my daughter with my words and with my actions. Confessing my sin to God and to Beth, I was well on my way into my spiritual U-turn. I began to compile a list of Beth's strengths and sweet personality traits:

She's kind and soft-spoken—even when provoked.

She is spending time with believers and reading her Bible.

She's a hard worker, keeping her room perfectly, cooking for her dad when I am gone, doing her homework carefully.

She is punctual, honest, generous . . . There were so many things.

How could I have been so blind? I made it a point to affirm her as often as I could. God had made His purpose clear to me.

I began to experience more of His power, the more and more I chose to obey. What was awkward for me at the beginning became natural for me. That's what God does. It's like the river Kathy talks about that has been flowing the wrong way a long time. You have to take the stones, one by one, and place them in a different position to redirect it. Before you know it the river runs in a new way and becomes stronger until one day it flows naturally and freely. As I put into practice a less critical spirit and a more affirming one, the presence of the Lord was becoming stronger, not only in my own life, but also in my interactions with Beth. She was actually coming to me, and sitting down with me, and sharing what was happening in her life. One night Steve and I were having supper with Beth and Annie. It was great conversation. We all shared the strengths we had seen God develop in one another.

Beth said, "Mom is an encourager."

I nearly fell off my chair. "Me?" I thanked the Lord for pouring light into my darkness, for purifying the murkiness of my river. Now that river was pouring life over my daughter, and blessing both of us.

Will we disappoint others and ourselves? Will we often fail in areas we so desperately want victory? Of course we will. But every time we fail there is provision.

If we confess our sins, he is faithful and just and will forgive us our sins and purify us from all unrighteousness. (1 John 1:9)

How often must we confess? Every time we let sin pollute the river of life within us. And every time, God's forgiveness will scoop it out, purifying our water, making it shimmer like crystal, bringing strength and beauty wherever they flow.

There is another principle that can help to transform you into a radiant woman who loves well. This principle will allow Christ to pour His life into you. When you first hear it, it will not sound attractive. But when you truly embrace it, you will actually see the strokes of the Master creating a work of art. His masterpiece is you—and the colors will be breathtaking.

PRINCIPLE TWO:

TRANSFORMED
by DEATH

*I tell you the truth, unless a kernel of wheat falls to
the ground and dies, it remains only a single seed. But
if it dies, it produces many seeds.*

(JOHN 12:24)

If by the Spirit you put to death the
misdeeds of the body, you will live.

(ROMANS 8:13B)

CHAPTER 6

AUTUMN GLORY

(Kathy)

I t was October in Virginia, and I was visiting Ellie and her family. When I awakened one morning I found the house completely empty. Still in my pajamas, I savored the quietness as I made some coffee and sat down at the kitchen table facing a huge bay window, marveling at the breathtaking autumn scene. There were still many leaves on the trees, but just as many on the ground. Like a child, I began to count the colors outside the window: fifteen, twenty, thirty . . . Just when I thought I was done, another shade caught my eye—so many different greens, yellows, and reds. The most gifted painter couldn't possibly capture what God displayed that morning before my eyes.

All these brilliant colors made the yard look so alive. As I was admiring the picture outside the window, I was reminded that there was a process of dying going on. In the midst of the splendor, each leaf would soon fall, decay, and turn the color of death. In a month the trees would be bare, the ground barren. It would be hard to imagine the backyard vibrant with color again, but new life would emerge in the spring.

AN UNUSUAL INVITATION

Jesus Christ gives us many invitations. He invites us to relationship with Him, to "pleasant places," and to an eternal banquet. One of the mysteries of our faith is that with all the wonderful invitations, He also invites us to die. This is the part of our Christianity that is hard for the Christian and foolish to the world. There's no way around it:

> Christianity involves the cross.
> Without the cross there is no victory for the Christian.
> When God invites us to die, it is so a resurrection can come.

God is so clear. He says it in many ways and in many places:

> *If it [a kernel of wheat] dies, it produces many seeds.* (John 12:24c)
> *If we died with him, we will also live with him.* (2 Timothy 2:11)
> *I have been crucified with Christ . . . but Christ lives in me.* (Galatians 2:20)

An invitation to die. We aren't dying just for death's sake, we are dying to make room for new life. So often we run away from it. So often we'll squirm out of it. So often we don't believe it. Who wants to die on a cross without the hope that a stone will be rolled away? But we must believe God. He is not a liar. It was a very dark day at Golgotha two thousand years ago, but three days later there *was* a resurrection.

I had to laugh when Dee told me about a cartoon of Katherine Kuhlman praying over an overweight person and saying, "Be healed of obesity." How I wished that were the case in 1978. I would have loved it if, after I invited Jesus into my heart, I had awakened a new creation at my ideal weight. Instead it took work, it took discipline, it took dying to myself. But today I am in a place of rejoicing.

Most of the time glorious resurrections happen only with agonizing passions. There is no "joy ride" to holiness. Dying will most definitely be involved. Pain and suffering come with it too. The perfect example is Jesus Christ. His death brought redemption to the world. And it was costly. And how was Jesus able to face the Cross? It was His faith that God would come through for Him.

For the joy set before him endured the cross. (Hebrews 12:2b)

Again, when the Scriptures urge us to die to ourselves, it isn't to suffer for suffering's sake, as if that's the measure of a saint. It is for more glorious things: an abundant life and a passionate heart, intimacy with God and one another, peace that passes understanding, a complete joy—all the jewels that John promised in the beginning of his letter and more. Don't trade the glory of God in your life for anything!

COLOR ME GRAY

Believers who have not experienced the power of dying to themselves are about as vibrant as cement. Believers like this *want* to be happy (who doesn't?), but shades of gloom continue to color their days. They *want* to have victory over the sin that binds them, but the blackness of their sin always seems to overcome the light. They *want* to know peace, but are overwhelmed with the turbulent circumstances of life. They *want* to have joyful intimacy in their marriage, but somehow it eludes them. Sins like pride, anger, bitterness, or a drive for wealth and status may be consuming them in such a way that they are *more* miserable than those who don't know Christ. Once you've tasted and seen that the Lord is good, He will always be whispering, wooing you to the cross, because He knows your only hope for life is in death: death to self, death to sinful passions, and death to all that the world holds so dear. Until we die, we cannot live.

FREE INDEED

(Kathy) Believe me, I have a lot more dying to do, but I've seen what happens in the places where I have allowed God to take me to the cross. Chains have fallen, freedom has come, and the Spirit of the living God has breathed life into my soul and into the souls of others. I have greatly admired believers that have learned the secret of dying—individuals like Billy Graham, Mother Teresa . . . You can almost touch Jesus in their person because of

their God-centeredness, their way of speaking, their way of answering people in interviews. Many of us have had those dinner conversations where questions are asked such as, "Who would you consider to be your hero?" It doesn't have to be someone of international prominence. In fact, we love it when people say, "My mother, my sister, my friend . . ." The people we think of are people who are so filled with love and integrity that they leave a legacy that cannot pass away. They are the believers John is describing when he says, "The world and its desires pass away, but the man who does the will of God lives forever" (1 John 2:17).

(Dee) John lists the sinful chains that hold back the life of God in us: "the lust of the flesh, and the lust of the eyes, and the pride of life" (1 John 2:16 KJV). As a young woman, I struggled greatly with the lust of the eyes, for I was consumed with the desire to have a *Better Homes and Gardens* house. It amazed me that when I laid that ideal down, freedom followed—freedom from the controlling lust that divides families and freedom to pursue a meaningful life. In this last year, Steve and I each lost a parent, and that required going through their material possessions with siblings. What freedom there is in realizing that none of the furniture, clothes, or dishes matter because it *is* all going to pass away—so if our siblings want *any* of it, we can joyfully say, "Take it!" Remember how Jesus responded when two brothers came to Him quarreling about their inheritance? Basically He told them that they just didn't get it— they didn't understand what *life* was really about (Luke 12:13–15).

How do we die to ourselves and our sinful ways? It's a process, such as the one falling leaves go through. You don't wake up one morning and see a glorious autumn. No, it happens gradually. In early September you may see the tinge of red on a few leaves, then perhaps a whole tree, like a burning bush, amid the others. But one day the whole forest and hills are ablaze with color. It's the same way with us.

Freedom takes time. Good counsel, being immersed in God's Word, vigilance, and a day-by-day setting your hand to the plow bring freedom. In some cases, you will realize you are truly free. The chains are gone. In others, you may not be truly free until heaven, but the shackles are loosened, and there is hope instead of despair.

(Dee) I interviewed a friend who beautifully demonstrates how to be set free. Andrea's chains were chains that many think are too heavy to be broken, the chains of homosexuality. Yet today she bears the radiant colors of His love in her person, is very happily married, and is breathing life into others who are still cold and gray. Andrea is a living testimony of all that John has been promising will happen if we learn how to submit ourselves to Jesus. Andrea's story isn't just a story about breaking free from homosexuality. The principles that helped her could be applied to those in bondage to an eating disorder, a bad temper, greed, envy, laziness, a critical spirit, or any of the hundreds of addictions that go against God's will for us.

But there is another reason we want to tell you Andrea's story. There are certain areas where the church has sadly lacked compassion, where we have failed to love our brothers and sisters. For example, so often the church has failed to give true understanding and support to the innocent victim of divorce. How often we have prayed and wept with a woman who did not want the divorce, but her husband had another woman, or didn't want to live with a Christian, and abandoned and divorced her. Yet *she* is made to feel like an outcast in the church. Did you know that it *doesn't* take two to get a divorce? One can file, and even if the other contests it, it will only slow it down—it will not stop it. Recently I was invited to speak at a church where I was told they do not allow divorced people, no matter the circumstances, to be members! I could hardly believe what I was hearing. Because I am very close to someone who is an innocent victim of divorce, I felt a holy flame leap up in my heart. Why didn't some of the leadership in that body realize that there *are* innocent victims of divorce? How quickly we can exchange the love of God and His absolute truth for cruelty and the distortions of legalism. Likewise, Kathy has seen how often Christians ask a woman not to have an abortion, but then shame her if she gives her baby up for adoption. What are we thinking? We can almost hear John, the "Son of Thunder," as Jesus nicknamed him, looking down from heaven and roaring: "How can the love of God be in you?"

We are also prone to judge in an area where we have *never* struggled—whether it is with obesity, substance abuse, stealing, rebellious children, or marital problems. We tend to be compassionate only in the areas where we have had battles. We judge people from our own life experiences. But that's not the love of Jesus. When I was speaking in a woman's prison in Omaha recently, my dear friend Eunice, who is working with the female inmates, said: "Dee, behind every one of these women is a story that would break your heart. I truly believe that if I had suffered what they had I would have ended up behind bars as well."

We have also failed to love the person who is struggling with sins that are especially repugnant to us. Whereas believers may feel compassion toward the person struggling with alcohol or anorexia, too often there is condemnation toward those struggling with homosexuality. Jesus ate with prostitutes and thieves, and the Pharisees condemned Him. Are we going to be like the Pharisees?

When I wrote *The Friendships of Women*, I included the story of a woman who was delivered from a homosexual lifestyle. I received more mail and phone calls about that particular story, especially from women still in bondage, than about anything else in that book. They would tell me their stories, and weep, and even talk about suicide. I was often thousands of miles away, and so I would plead with them to get help, to talk to someone at their local church. Usually they would respond, "Oh no—I couldn't. They wouldn't want anything to do with me." Instead of compassion, they sensed fear and repulsion. John pleads with us to "realize that our life in this world is actually his life lived in us" (1 John 4:17 PHILLIPS). Jesus was compassionate, so we must be too.

Sometimes we get confused, thinking that if we love the one in chains we are condoning the sin. We think that if we move close, that if we listen, then we are allowing that person to feel better about their bondage, when in reality, listening with a compassionate heart can prepare that person to receive the truth of Christ.

What we want you to see in Andrea's story is that it was definitely a process, and Jesus was a mighty Rescuer for her, but Andrea had to do her part as well. The same is true for you, no matter your sin.

WHO WILL RESCUE ME?

The reasons for sexual addiction are many and varied, but the promise of breaking free (because with God all things are possible) is for *all*, no matter the reason for the sin. In Andrea's case, she had been sexually abused by her father from the age of seven. I cannot even imagine the horror for a child, though Andrea helps me to empathize:

> *I was living in terror and trauma twenty-four hours a day, knowing that at any moment I could be abused. I associated femaleness with weakness, because my dad was overpowering me, night after night, and my mother wasn't rescuing me.*

One of the ways strongholds of sin can come into our lives is through generational sins. Bad tempers, alcohol abuse, and sexual problems often can be traced back to the last generation, and each of us needs to be open to the Spirit of God so that we can see where we need to break free from our past. The weeds of generational sin choke out any possible good fruit in us. We need to first recognize the evil and then get the help we need, which usually involves good Christian counseling, reading Scripture, prayer, and accountability. Each of those bold actions is like the blow of an ax to the grasping weeds that threaten the life of God in us.

In Andrea's case, instead of getting counseling, instead of getting the help she needed to break free from her past, she simply tried to live a "normal life" in her own strength. She married, but she was repulsed by the marriage bed, and the marriage ended in divorce.

It was while Andrea was teaching at a university that she met a woman who really listened to her, sympathized with her wounds, and embraced her.

> *It felt so wonderful to have someone really care, really listen. An intensity came into our relationship that was exciting. I even thought,* Thank God she's not a man, or I'd be having an affair. *The sexual feelings began to come forth, and I constructed a rationalization. At that time, I was into Buddhism, so I told myself I was a man who had been reincarnated in a woman's body.*

Satan looped a chain around Andrea through generational sin, and then tightened that chain with the deceit of Buddhism.

DRAWN TO THE LIGHT

Andrea's story here takes a wonderful turn, for the parents of the woman with whom she was having an affair loved the Lord deeply. How would you respond if one of your children had a homosexual lover? This couple, who happened to be Catholic charismatics, prayed and loved Andrea into the kingdom.

They were wonderful Italians who always had room at their table for one more mouth to feed. They would invite me to church, and it was this wild born-again church—something I had never experienced in my life and didn't understand but there was something about it I loved. After church I'd come home with them and sit at their table and tell them about Buddhism and Taoism. They listened and simply showed me acceptance and the grace of God. It blew my mind.

I watched their joy, their love, and their trust in adversity. This was a family who struggled to make ends meet, and the dad worked three jobs so that the mom could stay at home with the five kids. When the last kid left, they finally could afford a brand-new car—a cheap red Chevette. Right after they got it, somebody ran a red light and plowed into them. They got it fixed, and it happened again. I mocked them, saying, "Is this how God takes care of you?" But they were absolutely confident of His love and knew that somehow it would all work out for the good. And though they looked like total fools, it stuck with me.

It was their prayers, their love, and their trust in God that provided the slow and widening light for Andrea. She put her trust in Christ and the affair with their daughter ended. For two weeks Andrea sailed along, believing what the preacher had said:

If you want to be set free, all you have to do is come to Christ.

Wouldn't that be sweet? But just as Kathy didn't wake up a size six the morning after she came to Christ, and I didn't wake up a terrific wife and mother, Andrea didn't wake up freed from her sexual addiction. The power was within her, but there was still sin in her members, and the battle raged on.

Though God wanted Andrea to be set free, she didn't know how to stop the cycle. She would sin, repent, and sin again. It was the struggle we have all experienced with some kind of sin, the struggle Paul described when he said:

> *When I want to do good, evil is right there with me. For in my inner being I delight in God's law; but I see another law at work in the members of my body, waging war against the law of my mind and making me a prisoner of the law of sin at work within my members. What a wretched man I am! Who will rescue me from this body of death?* (Romans 7:21–24)

OUR PART

God is on our side. We must keep wrestling with Him, the way Jacob did. Andrea kept crying out to Him.

> *I was reading testimonies from those who had been set free. I remember in one book the author said that when we sin, whatever it is, we are being cannibals. We are eating others alive, destroying their hearts. That image stayed with me. I read that book when I was having my third affair. In my first two affairs, the women meant something to me. Now it was just a "summer fling." I was just using this woman because of my addiction. I was becoming my father. I was a cannibal: destroying another person in order to feed my flesh.*

The "cannibal" image portrays *the heart* of what John's letter teaches. If we do not walk in the light, if we do not die to ourselves, *we end up destroying our brothers.* Instead of becoming like God, who gives life, we become like our enemy, who was a murderer from the beginning.

God didn't give up on Andrea. Just as Hosea kept going after Gomer, the Lord kept going after Andrea. One passage He kept showing her through sermons and through friends was from Ezekiel, which pictures a baby abandoned by her parents:

> *Then I passed by and saw you kicking about in your blood, and as you lay there in your blood I said to you, "Live!" I made you grow like a plant of the field. You*

grew up and developed and became the most beautiful of jewels. Your breasts were formed and your hair grew, you who were naked and bare. (Ezekiel 16:6–7)

Though Andrea had been abandoned and abused as a child, God cared about her, and longed for her "to live!" One friend said to her:

Andrea, I see you crouched in a fetal position, in the back of a cold damp cave, but God's desire is for you to live!

This is His desire for each of us, to be transformed, to truly live. His Spirit continued to wrestle with her, speaking truth to her. Andrea said:

One night the Lord spoke to me. He said, "What would your obituary say? How diminished your life is. What gods are you serving?"

That was the moment Andrea stopped choosing to sin. God had spoken to her many times and in many ways, but that was the turning point. After that pivotal moment, she never returned to her sin. That's not to say her life was without temptation, but that she kept moving higher and higher up the ladder, closer and closer to the light.

I began to dialogue with God, asking Him what was His part? What was my part? It was a very sweet time, and just as God hedged Gomer in for a time, so that she couldn't sin, there was a period of nine months when God simply protected me from temptation while I began to get stronger. It was amazing grace.

I knew I had to keep His truth pouring into my soul. I read The Living Bible *in the format of* The Life Application Bible *and just kept dialoguing with God, asking Him to show me, to help me.*

One analogy that has been helpful to us is that God's truth is like the sap that rises in the spring, bringing new life to the trees. There are always those *stubborn* leaves that have refused to die, that have tenaciously clung to the branches all winter, but when the sap rises in the spring, it pushes them off.

The truth of God's Word can have the same effect. Whatever our struggle is, the same questions need to be asked. What is my part? What is God's part? What light can God's Word shed on this? The same questions apply whatever your struggle happens to be. Andrea continues:

> *A passage that became very meaningful to me was Romans 12:1–2. I began to realize I could really have the mind of Christ, that He could be incarnated through me, and that was so exciting. It also said,*

> *Then you will learn from your own experience how his ways will really satisfy you.* (Romans 12:2c TLB)

This truth that Andrea discovered is terribly significant. The reason we are unwilling to die to something is because we don't believe that God's ways can truly satisfy us. Do you see that in the above verse? John Piper, in *Desiring God*, pleads:

> *Take all your self-love—all your longing for joy and hope and love and security and fulfillment and significance—take all that and focus it on God, until he satisfies your heart and soul and mind. This is not a canceling out of self-love. This is a fulfillment of self-love . . . God says, "Come to me and I will give you fullness of joy" (Psalm 16:11) . . . And with that great discovery—that God is the never-ending fountain of our joy, the way we love others is forever changed.*[1]

Men are prone to make idols of their careers and accomplishments. Women, as the relational sex, are particularly vulnerable to making people their idols. Women can easily make their husbands, children, or friends their idols, expecting them to fill their deepest needs and to never let them down. So often we'll go through our days lifting a cup in the air saying, "Fill me, fill me." We have so many soul needs. But only Jesus can truly satisfy us. He calls to us, saying:

> *Open wide your mouth and I will fill it . . . with honey from the rock I would satisfy you.* (Psalm 81:10b, 16b)

Instead of using people or your position in life to get the love you want, find it in God, and in His pleasure in you. You can become a woman who loves well, who loves not to try to fill up her deep voids, but who is allowing the overflowing love she has found in God to spill out to others. Instead of loving from a needy heart, she loves from a full heart, for she has found a full joy.

LOVING FROM A FULL HEART

So often our area of ministry becomes the area where we have been set free. Andrea began counseling those still in the chains of homosexuality. One weekend Andrea went to a leaders' conference on sexual addictions. Rich was there, representing a ministry in Philadelphia. When Andrea walked in, Rich noticed her immediately. He said:

> *She was striking. Her countenance was one of confidence. Unfortunately, a lot of the people who are in leadership in this field still have a lot of woundedness. She was different. I wondered, Who is she?*

Unbeknownst to Andrea, Rich had prayed that if he were ever to marry, it would have to be someone who had been delivered from homosexuality, for she would truly be able to understand *where* he had been and *how* he had been set free. Though John 8:36 promises that "if the Son sets you free, you will be free indeed," many doubt that it can really happen in the area of homosexuality. So Rich longed for someone who *knew*, from her own experience, the *reality* of that freedom.

And unbeknownst to Rich, Andrea had told friends that if she were ever to marry, she wanted it to be someone standing clear on the other side of homosexuality, who was truly free. She longed for a husband who was willing to be a missionary, helping those still in bondage. Andrea watched Rich in amazement, seeing his heart for the lost, seeing his desire to be a father to the fatherless, seeing his great joy in the Lord. Rich watched Andrea, seeing her compassion, her wisdom, and her ability to articulate so clearly and so sensitively the truths of God. Rich and Andrea soon found themselves spending a lot of time together. Andrea said:

Our courtship was a beautiful drawing together—there were not lights and whistles at first, but a relationship founded in Christ. It really wasn't about us. It was about God. He was drawing us together. We each were truly content in our singleness, yet it was so clear that God was drawing us together.

One night I was at a conference called Living Water and a woman prayed a prophetic prayer over me, saying, "God is awakening you."

Shortly after that Rich and I definitely began coming out of our deep sleep.

FREEDOM FLYING

Andrea said that on her wedding day she flew into the heavenlies, and she hasn't landed. Andrea and Rich are a picture of innocence restored, of captives set free. Andrea glowed as she said:

When I was a little girl, probably just four, somebody told me enough about Jesus that I would pretend He was with me, playing with me in a grove of pine trees, running about and laughing with me. Now, in a beautiful way, I feel like I have my playmate again, and I am free and innocent, like a child.

Beautiful things happen on the other side of dying. There is an unspeakable joy and a sweet contentment in being right with God. Oftentimes, when healing occurs through a great trial or release from sin, the Lord brings us into a mighty place of ministry. That doesn't necessarily mean on an altar or a stage—it may happen in your own backyard, or within your family.

Isn't it interesting that so many of God's faithful men and women had sinned greatly? Moses was a murderer, Rahab a harlot, and Noah a drunk— yet God set them free and brought them into a place of enormous ministry. Today they are remembered, not for their sin, but for their faith in a God who can do the impossible.

THE HEBREWS HALL OF FAITH

God honors those who die to themselves and fully trust Him. They are indeed precious in His sight, and He describes many of them in Hebrews 11.

Take a brief journey with us to see the principle of dying in each of these individuals, and how through it, God brought new life, like the glorious colors of spring.

Abraham waited so long for his son Isaac. Sarah was old and had been barren for years. If anyone had a reason to cling too tightly to a child and to worship him, Abraham did. Yet though Abraham deeply loved his wife and his son, his source of fulfillment was God. He delighted in God, he trusted that God would do what was best for his loved ones, and so he obeyed God. When the Lord told him to sacrifice Isaac, he headed out to obey. Oh, to have that immediate and passionate response to the Almighty!

THE ANGEL STOPPING
ABRAHAM FROM
SACRIFICING ISAAC

REMBRANDT (1606–1669)

(Dee) As a parent, I simply cannot imagine doing what Abraham did. But sometimes God puts us in a situation where we simply don't have a choice. I waited a long time to have a daughter, and Sally is as dear to me, I believe, as Isaac was to Abraham. When Sally became a woman she moved to the

other side of the world and I had a terrible time releasing her and trusting that she was going to be all right. Though I knew of some very hard things in her life, including persecution for her faith, I realized that I was helpless to protect her. I *had* to abandon her to God. I had to trust He loved her more than I did, and that He would do all things well in His time. I had to trust that even if my worst fears for my daughter happened, that God was in control, and that He loved her. After several years I had a moment that I call my "Isaac" moment where I truly relinquished her to God.

Then I saw God intervene in Sally's life. He has been my daughter's faithful protector, provider, and rescuer. Once again I see that I belong to a God who is alive, who intercedes, and who is faithful.

Abraham was actually willing to sacrifice Isaac. Look carefully at what made him willing:

> *Abraham reasoned that God could raise the dead, and figuratively speaking, he did receive Isaac back from death.* (Hebrews 11:19)

Do you see the amazing faith in the above verse? Abraham truly believed that after he sacrificed Isaac that God would raise him from the dead! Frankly, we can't even imagine having that kind of faith. What trust, and what a beautiful picture of believing that from death would come life. Do you remember God's response? After He stopped Abraham from sacrificing Isaac, He said:

> *I swear by myself, declares the LORD, that because you have done this and have not withheld your son, your only son, I will surely bless you and make your descendants as numerous as the stars in the sky and as the sand on the seashore . . . All nations on earth will be blessed, because you have obeyed me.* (Genesis 22:16–17a; 18)

Not only did God see that Abraham trusted Him, but that Abraham loved God even more than he loved his son. What a challenge for us as mothers, for we are knit with our children! Yet God is worthy of that kind of first love.

(Kathy) I am inspired by the stories of Joseph and Moses, and how both refused "to enjoy the pleasures of sin for a short time" (Hebrews 11:25). Refusing to enjoy the "pleasures of sin"—a choice. What a war the flesh wages against the spirit! As long as I breathe I will deal with my passions and have to continually die to the ones that are not directed toward God. For example, during the height of my struggle with bulimia there were many days when I craved sweets and salt and would go from Oreos to French fries and back to Oreos . . . It would definitely have an effect on my body and my emotions the next day: I'd get bogged down; my ambition went out the window; I became a slug. There was a continual challenge every day for me to "choose the next right thing," to look at the reasons why I was "stuffing my body." Even though there was momentary pleasure, it robbed me of joy, of a healthy self-esteem in God, and of living in a sober state of being at peace with the Lord. We must constantly die to the momentary pleasures that throw us into darkness.

There are always sexual temptations for a single woman, as I'm sure there are for married women too. I must continually die to immediate gratification. I often think of Joseph's words when Potiphar's wife was inviting him to commit adultery: *How could I do this great sin against God?*

It helps greatly when I continually stay in the light by being accountable to those closest to me. Regarding obedience to God, Beth Moore has told me that I need to "plan my victories." This is what saved Joseph from sin.

Joseph was faithful to God and refused the evil woman's tempting, saying to her:

> *My master has withheld nothing from me except you, because you are his wife. How then could I do such a wicked thing and sin against God?* (Genesis 39:9)

This makes me think about my responsibility to live faithfully for Christ and to be an ambassador of the gospel. If I fall, how many women would be hurt who are looking to me? So when tempted I must ask, "*Why* would I do this great sin?" We must be aware of the consequences of our choices and cling to the Lord as our protection, our fortress against the enemy.

Perhaps you are not struggling with adultery, let's say, but with sinful

JOSEPH AND
POTIPHAR'S WIFE

ORAZIO GENTILESCHI
(1563 – 1639)

habits in a different area. It could be pride, the sin that always heads His list
of abominations. It could be watching ungodly programs on TV, being
judgmental of people, speaking harshly, or abusing your body by overeat-
ing. If you ask God to show you what grieves His heart the most in you, He
will. Ask Him to show you *where* to begin. Then ask Him to help you plan
a strategy for victory. He promises that if we ask for wisdom, He will give it
(James 1:5).

Denying yourself is never fun, but it will lead to a harvest of righteousness. The heroes of the faith believed God would be faithful to reward them
if they denied themselves the "pleasures of sin." We particularly like the passage where God brags a little bit about Moses' faith:

> *By faith Moses, when he had grown up, refused to be known as the son of
> Pharaoh's daughter. He chose to be mistreated along with the people of God rather
> than to enjoy the pleasures of sin for a short time. He regarded disgrace for the sake
> of Christ as of greater value than the treasures of Egypt, because he was looking
> ahead to his reward. By faith he left Egypt, not fearing the king's anger; he perse-
> vered because he saw him who is invisible.* (Hebrews 11:24–27)

Think about the "treasures in Egypt" you are tempted to worship.
Nothing can compare to delighting in God. If you are willing to die to

worldly pleasures and find your delight, instead, in God, He *will* give you fullness of joy and He will provide you "boundary lines in pleasant places."

GOOD TREES, GOOD FRUIT

One of the pleasant places He will lead you to is helping others still in darkness. The light God has given you can and should be passed on to others. He frees us and then uses us to free others.

(Dee) When I was set free from the selfishness that was destroying my marriage, I shared my story. More than once I had the joy of seeing other marriages set free. What delight it gives me today, to see their *children* walking with God, involved in full-time ministry, loving their husbands, and raising their own children in the nurture of the Lord. I identify with John when he wrote:

> *It has given me great joy to find some of your children walking in the truth . . .*
> (2 John 4)

Trust and dying to self transformed one of our favorite women in Scripture: Queen Esther. Esther was drastically changed from a woman who wanted to hide, like the chameleon who fades into his background, to a woman who put on her royal robes and took a stand. She trusted God and was filled with His power, wisdom, and strength. Esther was changed from a woman who feared death more than anything to a woman who was willing to lay down her life for her people. It is a story of redemption, a story of a woman who was transformed by the truth of the living God.

Pride goes before destruction, a haughty spirit before a fall.

(PROVERBS 16:18)

CHAPTER 7

IT'S NOT EASY BEING GREEN

(Kathy)

I love living in Nashville part of the year. I've often said I think Tennessee is one of the most beautiful states. It is so green—from its lush valleys to its densely forested mountains. In the spring the branches are bursting with new buds and thick green leaves, and in the fall the colors are absolutely magnificent. During these seasons I often take drives and marvel at God's creation.

Dee and I recently discovered something interesting about the color in leaves. The powerful green of the chlorophyll dominates the whole leaf. It thrives in warm weather and hides all the other glorious colors in the leaf. But in the autumn, when the weather turns cool, the chlorophyll *dies* and all the colors that have been hidden can be seen.

In the same way, God has created beautiful characteristics in each of us that He desires to see flourish. Those qualities can easily be hidden, like the colors in a leaf, if the overbearing "green" of pride dominates our person. But when we *die to our pride*, the beautiful colors of God's love can be seen.

So, though green *is* one of God's most beautiful and lush colors, in this chapter, we'd like you to associate it with the negative characteristic of pride. Ironically, the world values pride and exalts trusting in oneself, but when God lists the sins that are an abomination to Him, pride tops the list:

I [the Lord] *hate pride and arrogance . . .* (Proverbs 8:13)

There are six things the LORD hates, seven that are detestable to him:
   haughty eyes . . . (Proverbs 6:16–17a)

Why is pride an abomination to the Lord? Pride is what caused Satan to fall. Pride shuns trust in God and instead relies on self. C. S. Lewis called it the chief sin because it leads to all the others. When we say, "It's not easy being green," we are treading much too lightly. Pride will cause us great pain and suffering:

Pride will keep us from intimacy with God.
Pride will keep us from sweet fellowship with others.
Pride will rob us of genuine joy.
Pride kills, steals, and destroys.

PRIDE HIDES THE COLORS OF HIS LOVE

(Dee) After my sister Sally and I became Christians we began to share our faith with our sister Bonnie. Her defenses were always up because her siblings were "born again." Sometimes during my discussions with her, she would bring up controversial issues. She felt Christians were closed-minded and arrogant. Instead of listening to Bonnie and just letting her air her opinions, I would be argumentative, bringing her stereotypes to life. I was a bit haughty to say the least. Solomon says, "Pride leads to arguments" (Proverbs 13:10a TLB).

How vital it is to keep talking to God about ourselves. It allows God a say when you dialogue with Him, asking Him questions like: *How do You feel about my relationship with this person?*

I remember praying and asking Him: *What is the wall I see Bonnie putting up toward You? Why does she seem so closed?*

Much to my surprise, God's Spirit told me the answer.

You guessed it. *I* was the wall. She couldn't see God over my own arrogance and agenda. I was a large part of the reason Bonnie wasn't considering Jesus seriously.

Genuinely broken, I went to Bonnie and said: "I've been obnoxious. I haven't listened to you about things that are really important to you. Please forgive me, Bonnie. I promise you, you are going to see a different sister."

For the next few years I was very conscious of showing her the love of Christ. The wall between us began to crumble. You see, I really loved my sister, it's just that my pride, like the chlorophyll, hid the beautiful colors that He wanted to display before her.

The gospel can be so attractive, but how often we make it unattractive because we get in the way of the Good News. As I humbled myself, as I died to my pride, God's colorful love began to show through me, and I could sense that Bonnie's heart was growing tender. I knew she was more inquisitive about my faith. One summer she said, "Dee, I've never heard you speak. Are you going to be anywhere near Utah this year?" Bonnie flew to Idaho to hear me speak that following February. When I asked if anyone wanted to know Jesus, I saw my sister's hand go up. You can only imagine how I felt.

(Kathy) I had a similar experience of dying to pride when I committed my life to Jesus. I was going to colleges, career groups, and Christian coffeehouses. One particular group was planning a day for us to do some "street ministry." When they started talking about this, all I could think of was the man on the street corner in New York City. He would stand on his box with his microphone and amplifier and shout:

"Repent! Jesus saves!"

Some of these people mean well, but when I was young I always thought they were "a bunch of loonies." I'd just put my head down and quickly walk by. So now this whole idea of street ministry made me pretty uncomfortable. I'm an extrovert, so the idea of talking to people didn't scare me. But *this kind* of talking to people made me uneasy. However, because everyone else seemed so excited about it, I put my uneasiness aside and thought: *Okay, maybe this is the Christian thing to do.*

We went out to Southampton on Long Island. The Hamptons are charming—close to the ocean, with lovely bed and breakfast inns, shops, and eateries. Even now I look forward to spending time there. But this particular day I was dreading stepping out of the car. We all joined on a corner and then split up. Some of my friends were eager to talk to people, but I felt paralyzed.

We all have different gifts. I've definitely seen the Lord use this kind of "witnessing." Certain people have the gift of being able to hand out tracts, or to just walk up to people they've never met and engage them in a conversation about God. But none of us are poured through the same mold. Paul shared the gospel in a way that was different from John's way, Mark's way, or Stephen's way. But no matter how we communicate God's love, we all need to approach people respectfully, being full of His compassion for them.

I felt like I was back on the recital stage waiting for the curtain to open. Then I started shuffling my feet and decided to just "go for it." I saw two young women in their late twenties or early thirties sitting on a bench. I did what I had been taught to do, saying something like: "Do you guys know Jesus?"

One of them immediately responded with anger in her eyes and sharpness in her tone:

> "You know what? You people are all the same. You just get in everyone's face with your agendas. You think everybody is supposed to believe what you believe. Why don't you do something else with your time?"

Her abrasiveness startled me. I could hardly move. I must have looked like a deer caught in headlights. I found myself staring at her with my mouth open . . . and I started to weep. Then I plopped myself next to them and let out the biggest sigh.

> "Hey listen . . . I'm feeling so stupid. I'm sorry. This isn't me. This isn't my style. I've got to tell you I used to think the same way you do about Christians. That's why I had trouble even going with my group today.
>
> "I'm uncomfortable because I know I don't know you and you don't know me. I've just recently come to know who Jesus really is and I just want others to know Him because He's wonderful."

As I spoke my true heart the two girls were sweet enough to stay and their countenances softened as we talked. We each shared about our lives. By the time I got up they said they were interested in visiting my church. We hugged good-bye.

When we are willing to die to our pride, to our agenda, and to humble ourselves by being honest, then glorious colors, like the colors of autumn leaves, can come forth. People will come to God, friendships will be cemented, marriages will thrive, joy will bubble up, and peace will flow. No wonder John tells us to die to "the pride of life." Pride is fleeting, and gives a momentary exaltation, but then all comes crashing down. With humility come honor, wisdom, and the things that can never pass away.

Esther and the Wizard of Oz

One of our favorite movies is *The Wizard of Oz*. Every once in a while we'll watch the video of this wonderful story of friendships in a magical land. Remember how it begins in black and white? Dorothy is at her Auntie Em's in Kansas, and the farm, the landscape, and life itself seem dreary. Dorothy longs for a more exciting life in a land "Somewhere Over the Rainbow."

A tornado suddenly sends the house and Dorothy swirling. Hitting her head, she begins to dream, and suddenly she and Toto are in the colorful Land of Oz. The dull blacks and whites disappear. Dorothy skips down a yellow brick road toward an emerald castle. An evil witch with a shocking green face appears. A good witch gives Dorothy a pair of ruby red slippers. What a change from Auntie Em's farm in Kansas! All this is symbolized by a transformation to Technicolor.

If we were to make a movie of the book of Esther, we would use a similar technique. In the beginning of this book the central characters, Esther and her guardian, Mordecai, who are Jews, seem to be operating on the basis of arrogance and fear. Instead of aligning themselves with God, they hide their colors of faith. Mordecai also engages in a prideful dispute with the king's right-hand man, Haman. Instead of being vibrant with the life of God, Mordecai and Esther are faded. Instead of shining like stars amid a crooked and perverse generation, they act like chameleons, those ugly little lizards that take on the dull grays, greens, or browns of their background, so that no one will notice them. Yet later in the book, when faced with an edict for a holocaust against Jews, there is a change. Instead of pride, there is sackcloth and ashes. Instead of fear there is courage. Instead of being conformed to their world, they are transformed by the truth of God. Instead of clinging to their lives they are willing to lay them down. This is when we would symbolize the wonderful transformation in God's people by turning the movie from black and white to Technicolor.

Many who have written or described the book of Esther have glossed over the beginning, the embarrassing part when the believers were not living distinctive lives. Or they have simply failed to see it, for the story is told with extreme subtlety. History has often put Esther and her guardian, Mordecai, on pedestals. If those relating the story saw their feet of clay, they discreetly covered them. How we long to have heroes and heroines with no flaws.

But that's not real life.

Just as we are in a process, just as we are learning to yield ourselves to the Lord, the same was true with Esther and Mordecai. There are also many Bible historians who *have* seen the flaws in the believers in Esther. John MacArthur asks, in his introductory remarks to the book of Esther, "Why were Mordecai and Esther so secular in their lifestyles?" Why did they not "seem to have the same kind of open devotion to God as Daniel?"[1]

(Dee) Perhaps the most controversial study guide I have ever written is *A Woman's Journey through Esther.* I have received so much encouraging mail about this guide, but a few letters have been angry. One woman wrote:

> *Esther has always been my heroine. How could you say the things you did about her? We won't be purchasing your guides anymore.*

Many have not looked deeply into the story of Esther, but we must. It may be appropriate for "VeggieTales" to skip the decadent sexual immorality in Esther, but it is not for us. We must see these people as they really were. For many, especially the Jews, Esther and Mordecai have become objects of adulation. When the book of Esther is read among the Jews at their holiday of Purim, the children boo when Haman's name is read and cheer loudly whenever Esther's or Mordecai's name is read. Considering the enormous suffering of the Jewish people, it is understandable that Esther, who risked her life for her people, would be a heroine. And she is! She came to exemplify exactly what John says real love is, when he says just as Jesus laid down His life, so are we to lay down our lives for our brothers (1 John 3:16). She came to be that shining "star" that the name "Esther" means.

FRESCO OF ESTHER

ANDREA DEL CASTAGNO
(1423–1457)

However, it is also vital to see the *whole* story as it really happened, and to see that Esther and Mordecai were not such wonderful role models in the beginning. I have also received many letters from those who have thanked me for encouraging them to dig deeper, and to see things they had not seen before. One woman wrote:

> *Instead of discouraging me, seeing how Esther failed to withstand the pressures of her world in her youth has actually encouraged me. Seeing how God is a God of second chances, and how He redeemed that whole situation has given me enormous hope. I failed. Though I was a believer I had premarital sex and then an abortion. Thousands of times I have wished I could undo my sin. But I cannot. This story has given me hope that though my sin grieved the heart of God, He*

still can turn ashes into beauty, if I trust Him and obey Him the way Esther learned to do.

The book of Esther causes controversy for several reasons. It isn't unusual for a hero to fail, for Moses, David, and Peter all failed. What *is* unusual is for God to be silent about the failure. When David sinned, we are told, "the thing David had done displeased the LORD" (2 Sam. 11:27b). But in Esther, not only is God silent, His name is not even mentioned, the only book in the whole Bible with that distinction. F. B. Huey Jr., in *The Expositor's Commentary,* explains that "the hiddenness of God can sometimes be explained as evidence of His displeasure (Amos 8:11, Ezekiel 11:23)."[2] God's silence adds to the mystery and the controversy of Esther, for the reader is left to decide if Vashti was right to disobey her husband, if Esther was right to participate in the beauty contest, and if Mordecai and Esther were right to hide their faith.

How do we decide right and wrong when it comes to moral issues? Do we decide on the basis of what feels right, or what works well in the end? Neither. We decide on the basis of didactic, or teaching, principles from God's Word, often clearly stated in the New Testament. For example, we are clearly told: "Flee from sexual immorality" (1 Corinthians 6:18). Therefore, we know that even though the pressure was enormous, it wasn't right for Esther to participate in this immoral contest.

But how can we *not* be sympathetic to Esther? She was alone, vulnerable, and probably quite young. She obeyed Mordecai, as she had always done growing up. We cannot know, for certain, why the two of them made such choices. John MacArthur states, "This issue must ultimately be resolved by God since He alone knows human hearts."[3] Our God is a God of grace, and He knows things we cannot, in our limited vision, know.

(Dee) Yet unless we look carefully at Scripture, we may miss the truth. Then, upon that false perception, we will make erroneous applications. I've cringed upon hearing some of the advice given to young women based on a misunderstanding of what was actually happening in the book of Esther. Seeing the truth often means slowing down and looking carefully—not only

at context, but also at culture and history. With Esther, enormous light is shed by going back three generations.

Often the sins that bind us are generational sins. Breaking free means understanding the power of the past over our lives. In Esther's case, *three* generations before these events occurred, we can see that the faith of *that* generation was strong, but then there was moral decay, with each succeeding generation reflecting less of God in their lives.

THE FAITH OF OUR FATHERS

Nearly 120 years before Esther, Nebuchadnezzar destroyed Jerusalem and took many Jews into captivity. Among them was Mordecai's great-grandfather Kish. The most famous captive was Daniel. Daniel had the courage to refuse the king's order to cease praying to the Lord, and trusted God with his life. Nebuchadnezzar threw Daniel into the lions' den. Courageously Daniel trusted God, and God's Spirit fell upon the lions and caused them to shut their mouths.

DANIEL IN THE DEN
OF LIONS

BRITON RIVIERE (1840–1920)

Daniel was also mentor to three young men, whom we have come to know as Shadrach, Meshach, and Abednego. When the king asked them to do something immoral (bow down to a gold idol) they too refused. Here they are descending into the fiery furnace, willing to face death to do what was right in the sight of the Lord:

THE FIERY FURNACE FAILS

JAMES TISSOT (1836–1902)

All of these believers were willing to die rather than compromise their faith. They believed the Lord would deliver them, but it is significant to see that "even if He did not," they would not compromise. Look carefully at their response to Nebuchadnezzar, and remember it, for their undying faith reveals a sharp contrast to the way the believers in the opening of Esther responded to pressure.

> *If we are thrown into the blazing furnace, the God we serve is able to save us from it, and he will rescue us from your hand, O king. But even if he does not, we want you to know, O king, that we will not serve your gods or worship the image of gold you have set up.* (Daniel 3:17–18)

THE EMPTY WAY OF LIFE OF OUR FOREFATHERS

The succeeding generations were not alive with this kind of faith. God has also given us these stories as a warning. Fifty years before Esther, Cyrus released the Jews from captivity, giving believers the freedom to return to the Holy Land. Many left, but some chose to stay. Did they stay in order to be missionaries in this pagan land? The evidence is strong that this was *not* their motive. Instead it seems they had become comfortable, conformed to their surroundings, and unconcerned about returning to their people. Commentator John Brug says that the book of Esther is deliberately written in the style of a Persian secular narrative to reflect the conditions and attitudes of Jews scattered in Persia in contrast to those of dedicated Jews in the Holy Land.[4] John tells us, "Love not the world." But the immediate ancestors of Esther and Mordecai seemed to love the pleasure of Persia. Their lives had been conformed to the world around them, and they handed this empty way of life down to the next generation. So it is not surprising that the believers in Esther, at least in the beginning of the story, were reflecting the faded colors of their immediate ancestors.

Though it took place thousands of years ago, the world of ancient Persia was uncannily like the evil world in which we live, a world consumed with wealth, illicit sex, and entertainment.

PUFFED UP WITH PRIDE, POWER, AND POSITION

The story begins with a six-month party. It's hard to imagine, isn't it?

The guest list was made up of the military leaders of Persia. Xerxes' party was designed to impress them and persuade them to invade Greece. Xerxes thought that if he could conquer Greece, he would be king of the whole world. If we were to make a comic book of Esther, Xerxes would look like the Jolly Green Giant (without the jolly). He was puffed up with his own power and importance. But he wasn't a comic book villain—he really lived, and history is filled with stories of his cruelties. Because of pride, Xerxes often shed innocent blood, whether it was to add to his domain, to do away with a wife who displeased him, or to demonstrate that *nobody* defied the king. The historian Herodotus reports that Pythius of Lydia, an extremely wealthy man, offered to finance the war. The elderly statesman had one small favor to ask of Xerxes, and that was that the eldest of his five sons be allowed to stay at home. When the men left for war, Xerxes had the eldest son of Pythius cut in half. The army marched to war between the halves of the young man's corpse. He said to Pythius, "There, now you can keep your son at home."⁵ Xerxes certainly reflected the heart of his father, Satan.

Xerxes' party was more ostentatious than the most elaborate parties Hollywood has ever thrown. Even the weddings of the biggest stars would pale in comparison. It is also a party that exemplifies the things of evil and all of the distorted values that John tells us not to love:

> *the craze for sex,*
> *the ambition to buy everything that appeals to you,*
> *and the pride that comes from wealth and importance*
> (1 John 2:16 TLB)

The purpose of the party is clearly stated, in an almost blasphemous phrase:

> *For a full 180 days he displayed the vast wealth of his kingdom and the splendor and glory of his majesty.* (Esther 1:4)

Xerxes displayed his wealth and power for six months. When the six months were over, he ended it with a seven-day banquet in his enclosed garden. Nothing was held back: wine was served in elaborate golden goblets, the men reclined on couches of silver and gold, and the floor was a mosaic pavement of marble, mother-of-pearl, and other costly stones. (Archaeological excavations have substantiated this.) As with all things "under the sun," we can get used to them, and soon they are boring. The only way to keep interest alive is to escalate, and Xerxes wanted to end his party with a bang. So he called for his seven eunuchs to bring in his wife, Vashti. Eunuchs were men who had been castrated to guard the queen.

One way you can measure the decadence of a country is by the way it treats its people. How sad to castrate young men, robbing them of their manhood and their hopes for a family.

And why were seven men needed to bring in *one* woman?

It is possible Xerxes anticipated resistance. What woman would *want* to appear before a drunken stag party? It is also possible that the eunuchs were going to bring Vashti in on some kind of a platform. Some commentators say she was to wear only her crown (Esther 1:11). Josephus, one ancient historian, said she was to appear in the nude.[6] Whether or not this is correct, it is clear it was a demeaning request.

(Dee) It astounds me when I hear young women told that if they refuse their husbands, as Vashti did, they can also expect God's disapproval. I think, *If this speaker knew what was really being asked of Vashti, he (or she) would never say that. Would they tell women to submit to an orgy?* Although Scripture *does* tell us to submit to our husbands, there is one exception: if your husband asks you to do something that is blatantly against God's moral law, you must refuse. You should be gracious, but you should never submit to sin.

Whatever her motivation—and we do not know her heart, for it may have been virtuous or vindictive—Vashti refuses the order. The lights don't go on. The curtains don't go up. Instead of ending his party with a bang, Xerxes is humiliated. And his counselor Memucan, who has also been drinking without restraint, is extremely angry. He says:

> According to law, what must be done to Queen Vashti? . . . She has not obeyed the command of King Xerxes that the eunuchs have taken to her. (Esther 1:15)

The decision is made to banish Vashti. Some historians say she was deposed and others say she was beheaded. Her defiance, whatever motivated it, is very significant. Vashti took a stand—and she paid the cost. She is no longer queen. A new queen must be found.

IT'S NOT EASY BEING QUEEN

As time passes, Xerxes regrets going along with his counselors. He misses Vashti. Again, the counselors fly into action. Again, it is another cruel plan.

They suggest a contest to replace Vashti. Virgins will "be taken" from all 127 provinces, an area bigger than the United States. What will the qualifications be for the new queen? Wisdom? Character? An ability to rule her people with justice and compassion?

No. The only qualification was an ability to "please" the king (Esther 2:2–4). And how might that be? This is where you need to read carefully. The story is told with great subtlety and many have missed what is actually happening. When this story is told, so often the narrator makes a light-hearted comment about the twelve months of beauty treatments, leaps over the next dark passage, and abruptly announces: "Esther is the new queen!"

This was not a lighthearted beauty contest. Innocence was stolen, dreams were destroyed, and young women became slaves in an immoral kingdom.

For six months, each virgin had oil rubbed into her skin so she would be soft and touchable for the king. For another six months, she would try on various kinds of perfumes and cosmetics. Then, one by one, each virgin would go to the king in the evening. In the morning she would return to live, not with the virgins, but with the concubines. She would not return to the king unless he was pleased with her and called for her by name. (Esther 2:12–14).

Joyce Baldwin writes that though the twelve months of beauty treatments could be likened to a preparation for a bride, the sad thing is that for most, it was more a preparation for widowhood.[7] Most had one night and then became a slave in the kingdom. Any dreams for the future died if she failed to please the king. It was a terrible thing to do to young women, robbing them of their purity, their hopes for a family, or for a meaningful life.

Often the character of a country or a religion can be seen in its treatment of women. Josephus said that 400 virgins were involved.[8] Another historian estimates it was 1,460 (a virgin a night for four years).[9] Certainly it was an abuse of women. Imagine how you might feel if your daughter was taken to participate in this decadent contest.

Why did Esther's guardian, Mordecai, allow Esther to participate? Surely he knew that this kind of sexual immorality was a compromise to their faith. Some historians believe he was politically ambitious and thought she could win. That's one possibility. A more likely possibility is that he was operating out of fear. He seemed to be deeply concerned for her. His faith did not seem particularly strong, for though he lived in Persia for a long time, no one realized he was a believer. We propose that Mordecai feared for Esther's life, for he knew Xerxes' reputation for cruelty, and so he told her to do whatever it took to stay alive.

What did it take? Twelve months of treatments, lessons to learn how to please a lecherous king, and one immoral night with him. Let's not forget there were also seven years of pretending she was not a believer in the one true God.

Often people defend the poor choices of women in Scripture, saying they had to do whatever the men wanted them to do. Certainly the pressure was great. However, we are so thankful that God *has* given us models of women who resisted the evil pressure of their times. When the Hebrew midwives, for example, were told to kill the boy babies, they refused, and God was pleased, giving the midwives families of their own. When Abigail heard that her foolish husband Nabal was mistreating David, she flew into action. These women did not compromise with sin and God showed them mercy. (That is not to say that obedience will always lead to a happy ending. What it will definitely do is keep you in the center of God's will and fill you with a supernatural peace.)

Obviously the pressure on Esther was enormous. Xerxes was a capricious and cruel man. Still, it is important to contrast the choice that Esther made with the choice of Shadrach, Meshach, and Abednego. When they were taken against their will into an immoral kingdom and asked to compromise their faith, they refused, believing their God could deliver them. But even if He did not, they said they would not "bow down."

A key difference is that Shadrach, Meshach, and Abednego had Daniel as a mentor. Daniel had already modeled faith for them. Esther's only mentor seemed to be Mordecai, who had forbidden her to reveal her faith (Esther 2:10).

THE IMPORTANCE OF GODLY FRIENDS

(*Kathy*) My mother used to always say, "You are who you are around." There was a time in my life when I would roll my eyes at some of her tidbits of motherly wisdom. She lived in such close proximity to our extended family, and her whole life revolved around them. Although I loved my family, I would dismiss what she had to say, feeling she lived in such a sheltered little world. I would think, *Mom, give me a break. I'm just trying to branch out here.* But most of us, as we get older, realize that Mom and Dad weren't so dumb. It's true: "You are who you are around."

I see it all the time now. I see it with some of my friends. I see it with leaders in the church. I see it with my own family members. They may think that the friends they have chosen don't influence them, but they do. I've seen people who were once filled with zeal and a hunger and thirst for righteousness become almost complacent and apathetic toward the things that used to stir their souls toward holiness. The people they have aligned themselves with have caused them to "shut down" their journey. They decide to stop walking and sit down for a while. Making themselves "comfy," they eventually lie down. Before they know it they're all living together in a little valley somewhere far away from the mountains that they once wished to conquer. There is no longer any challenge to pick up the cross. That sounds dramatic but that kind of holy and sacred talk even becomes ridiculed.

It's like the progression in Psalm 1, from standing in the way of sinners to finally sitting in the seat of mockers, mocking at the things of God. The goal for living becomes more of a "let's not hurt anyone," "let's try to be good people," and "let's not judge anybody." I believe that kind of mentality sets in because that person no longer wants to be under the gaze of God Himself. Because when you allow God to look at you, He will judge you rightly, see you correctly, and challenge you to die so you can live. Where you once received the call to holiness you now just let the phone keep ringing or pick it up and quickly hang up.

(Dee) Our two oldest children, both sons, made some unwise choices in friendship as teenagers and went through a time of rebellion. God brought both of them back to Himself, and as men they have walked closely with Him. Yet if I had a second chance at raising them, I would definitely be more prayerful and proactive concerning their friends. Paul warns so severely:

Do not be misled: "Bad company corrupts good character." (1 Corinthians 15:33)

So when our third child, Sally, was in fifth grade, I was determined to learn from my mistakes. I prayed so for godly friends for her. During one of my prayer times, the Lord impressed on my heart that I should look for godly mothers who were doing a good job of discipling their fifth-grade daughters. He was so gracious to reveal them to me, one by one. They happened to be from different churches, races, and backgrounds, but they loved the Lord deeply and were eager to meet and to pray together for our daughters.

Precious friendships emerged. We prayed through Scripture, we prayed for their character, and we prayed for their relationships. It is so exciting to belong to a God who answers prayer. We saw our daughters begin to become friends and to encourage each other in their faith. Sally and Robyn became accountable to one another, asking each other what they were learning in their daily times with God. Sally said, "Robyn would wait for me each day outside of my English class and ask me what I had learned in my time with God. So I knew I had to learn something!" They were making choices different from those many of their peers were making in regard to music, video rentals, dress, dating, sex, and alcohol.

I'll come back to this story, for it was not as rosy as it sounds. We, as mothers, had a sharp disagreement at one point and nearly brought the good thing God was doing tumbling down. Pride nearly did us all in! Fanning the flames of pride seems to be one of Satan's favorite devices, for he has found it to be *very* effective down through the ages. In fact, this is how Satan nearly destroyed God's people in the book of Esther. Pride was Mordecai's besetting sin, though he knew the Lord.

MORDECAI, THE JEW

The author of the book of Esther makes a big point of identifying Mordecai as a Jew. But Mordecai was *not* bearing the beautiful colors of faith, humility, and gentleness. Instead, he was fearful, prideful, and even hateful. But, tongue-in-cheek, the author still keeps identifying him as Mordecai, the Jew.

You will also see that whenever Haman, who was the Hitler of Esther's day, is announced, it is usually, "Haman, the Agagite." Again, this is significant, and the author seems to be emphasizing the long-standing feud between the Jews and the Agagites.

Though Mordecai had lived outside the palace for seven years, no one knew he was a Jew. Perhaps you have heard the rhetorical question: "Would there be enough evidence to convict you of being a Christian?" Apparently there was not enough evidence to identify Mordecai as belonging to the one true God. Carl Armerding writes:

> *The fact that he had to tell others that he was a Jew is interesting* (Esther 3:4).
> *Apparently he had lived so long in Persia that he must have become like them.*[10]

When the people of the kingdom kept asking him *why* he was refusing to bow down to Haman, Mordecai finally admitted he was Jewish.

Again, Mordecai's refusal to bow down is controversial. Did Mordecai refuse to bow down in obedience to God? Was he following the example of his godly ancestors who refused to bow down to the golden idol? We think not. Showing honor to a man in government office is entirely different from worshiping a golden idol. Scripture gives many examples of godly people who bowed to their political superiors to show respect for the office God had ordained. We would liken it to an incident in recent history when a National Prayer Breakfast was held shortly after President Clinton was involved in a sexual scandal with Monica Lewinsky, a young intern. When the president walked into the room, most rose to their feet, but some believers refused to rise. We understand, but we believe that they should have stood in respect, not for the man, but for the office God had ordained. The evidence seems strong—as the author keeps accentuating the feud through the contrast of Mordecai the Jew and Haman the Agagite—that the motivation for the refusal lay in this long-standing feud. Frederic Bush, in the *Word Biblical Commentary*, writes:

> *Mordecai's action was one of ethnic pride. He simply would not bow down to*
> *a descendant of the Amalekites.*[11]

Some of you may think, *Well, I wouldn't bow down to someone like Hitler either*. But at this point in the story Haman had not asked for a holocaust against the Jews. He was simply an arrogant man in charge and an Agagite.

With Pride Comes Contention

(Dee) One day Satan nearly destroyed the prayer group that I had with other mothers. It began innocently, when one of the mothers suggested that we come up with a list of standards for our daughters. She suggested, for example, that R-rated movies be off-limits in all of our homes. It seemed like a good idea, but when we began to try to agree, we found we could *not* agree.

One mother said, "Of course they shouldn't watch R-rated movies. They shouldn't be watching PG-13 rated movies."

Another said, "They shouldn't be watching movies."

Another said, "Come on now, you're both being too legalistic."

The atmosphere began to change. The sense of a storm coming was in the air. We switched to another subject. Maybe we could find agreement on the subject of dating.

One mother said, "They shouldn't be dating before they are eighteen."

Another said, "They shouldn't be dating before they are sixteen."

Another said, "Come on, you guys, every individual is different."

Soon we were like mother bears, defending the territory of our young. You could almost hear the low growls. Tempers began to flare. Unkind words were spoken. Someone left in tears. Others followed. Eventually, only my friend Shell was left.

At that moment the usual affection I had for Shell dissipated. Instead of being quick to listen, slow to speak, and slow to become angry, I told her, in less than gracious words, that I thought she was much too strict with her daughters.

Shell walked out the door.

When this incident happened, I was right in the middle of writing *The Friendships of Women*. I told Steve that I didn't see how I could finish it, because all of my friends had just left in tears. How could I preach about women's friendships? I remember how he responded:

> "Could it be, honey, that God is trying to speak to you? I have heard you say that if there is a problem in a horizontal relationship, there is often a problem in your vertical relationship with God."

Steve was absolutely right. I called Shell. I was sincerely repentant and I pleaded with her to forgive me. But though she *said* she forgave me, she was cool. She stopped calling me. She stopped coming over. I thought, *I've done all I know to do. I've shown her that she is valuable to me*. Now my heart started turning. *Doesn't she realize what a precious friend she could be losing in me?* I began to want her to feel the hurt I was feeling.

When I told Kathy about this incident, and of how hard it was for me to just let it go, she said, in her usual honest and sympathetic way: "Dee, everyone could relate to that. You feel like, *What does she want me to do? Wash her feet?* I understand, Dee—you can get so exasperated when you are really truly sorry and someone doesn't forgive you." I knew that now *Shell* was the one wrong for not forgiving me, but instead of just giving it to God, I wanted to make my withdrawing from her obvious. I was embarrassingly guilty of "twisting the knife."

Mordecai found a way to stick the knife into Haman, and so he did. He simply would not bow, enjoying Haman's infuriation. I don't think he had *any* idea of the hurricane his prideful action was going to unleash. There was no way Mordecai's choice was going to be ignored. His "green" was going to invade their world like a growing mold. Pride and hate tend to escalate a feud, whereas love can stop it in its tracks. "Where there is no wood," Solomon tells us, "the fire goes out" (Proverbs 26:20 NKJV).

It is *so* difficult to die to pride.

But if we do, it is amazing what beautiful colors will emerge.

To be honest, if I had not been writing a book on friendship, a book about which I cared so deeply, I'm not sure I would have responded the way I did. But I wanted God's blessing so badly on that book that I knew I had to die to my pride and truly live out what I was writing about. My husband reminded me that sometimes *saying* you are sorry is not enough to mend a breach. Sometimes you have to bear fruit worthy of repentance.

So I wrote Shell a note telling her why I loved her. A few days later I took blueberry muffins to her home. When she opened the door, we fell into each other's arms and wept. She said, "Dee, I was going to forgive you, but just not quite yet." We laughed. What vain and silly creatures we are!

We also began to call the other mothers and plead for forgiveness. They were gracious, and the Lord brought us together again. I am convinced that one of Satan's primary strategies is to fan the flames of pride so that he can divide and scatter the sheep. He knows that dividing us dilutes our strength. He knows that the world looks on and scoffs at believers of a loving God not loving each other.

We have no doubt that Satan was behind the scenes in the story of Esther. Satan has always hated God's people and longed to wipe them out. Fanning the flames of pride has worked to help him cause discord time and time again.

Pride Goes Before a Fall

The feud between Mordecai the Jew and Haman the Agagite escalated. Haman was a man of overwhelming vanity, and Mordecai had touched his vulnerable spot. Haman goes to Xerxes and asks him to sign an edict for a holocaust. Killing only Mordecai would not satisfy him. He wants all of Mordecai's people wiped out. How does he convince Xerxes? Again, we see someone who reflects the cleverness of the father of lies. Notice how Haman never mentions that these "certain people" are the Jews. As he speaks about the Jews, he begins with a truth, then moves to a half-truth, and finally to an outright lie:

TRUTH:
> *There is a certain people dispersed and scattered among the peoples in all the provinces of your kingdom whose customs are different from those of all other people.* (Esther 3:8a)

This was the truth. The Jews were dispersed and had different customs.

HALF-TRUTH:

> . . . *and who do not obey the king's laws.* (Esther 3:8a)

This was a half-truth, for the Jews were law-abiding citizens. However, if the king asked them to defy God, there were Jews (like Daniel) who took a stand.

LIE:

> *It is not in the king's best interest to tolerate them.* (Esther 3:8b)

This was a bold-faced lie, for if you touch the Jews, the apple of God's eye, you can count on His wrath to fall on you. But because Haman has prefaced this lie with a truth and a half-truth, Xerxes has been lured into a net. (All of us have to be on guard for this kind of deception in our lives.) Then Haman sweetens his request with an enormous bribe. Xerxes lunges, and the net is secure. An edict is signed, the purim (die) is cast, and a date is set on which all the Jews, including women and children, are to be murdered.

Satan certainly used Haman to try to wipe out God's people, but we must not forget that *it was the pride of Moredecai* that provoked Haman's rage. Dr. Joyce Baldwin writes:

> *Mordecai, by his pig-headed pride or loyalty, brought disaster not only on himself, but on his whole race.*[12]

THE GOD OF SECOND CHANCES

How thankful we are that even when we've blown it, our Lord doesn't give up on us. That's why we call Him our Redeemer. When we are willing to die to our pride and to do what is right, no matter the cost, He can birth beauty in us.

That's what He did in the story of Esther. Though the believers were cold and colorless in the beginning of the story, by the time the edict for the holocaust is known, we sense the winds of change.

The pride that had so gripped Mordecai *dies*. He was a desperate man. By the beginning of chapter 4, we find Mordecai truly humbled. In sackcloth and ashes, he is wailing loudly. He knows he cannot handle this crisis alone. His arrogance is gone. He is turning to God with all his heart and his ugly green face, like the face of the evil witch in *The Wizard of Oz*, is transformed. No longer are his eyes haughty, but closed in earnest prayer. When Mordecai's pride dies, a glimpse of color can be seen, like that first red leaf that can be spotted in late August. But soon you see another, and another . . .

So it was in the book of Esther, as one Jew after another humbled himself, put on sackcloth, and pleaded with God for deliverance. As their pride dies, revival comes, sweeping across the land like the colors of autumn. And nowhere are those colors more brilliant or more beautiful than in the person of Esther.

TRANSFORMED
by TRUTH

Then you will know the truth, and the truth will set you free.

(JOHN 8:32)

This is how we recognize the Spirit of truth and the spirit of falsehood.

(1 JOHN 4:6B)

CHAPTER 8

TRUE BLUE

We have loved sharing the platform with women like Cynthia Heald, Jan Silvious, Beth Moore, and many others. We are so thankful for women of depth and substance who will boldly articulate the absolute truths of the Word of God.

(Dee) I have also loved sharing the platform with Kathy, for she is a deep soul. After the terrorist attacks on September 11, 2001, Kathy and I drove together to our speaking engagements for the following weekend. In the car we wept, prayed, and talked about what this tragedy meant in the eternal scheme of things. God's Spirit was giving Kathy words.

At that Saturday's events, many of the speakers *stayed* with their planned talks, with just a slight variation, because it *is* hard to change directions so quickly. But the women listening were not in the mood for canned talks or jokes. They were *yearning* to have what had just happened boldly addressed. When Kathy came out, she spoke spontaneously with the genuineness that drew me to her in the first place. Among the words that came from her passionate heart were:

My beloved city has lost so many souls. The drastically altered majestic skyline is a reminder of the presence of evil in this world. All I could do as I watched the

horror was cry out to Jesus. I begged for His mercy and I pleaded His blood upon
this nation as thousands lost their lives because of this horrific act. As the fire and
smoke were filling the skies over New York and Washington, D.C., I pictured what
was filling the skies in the heavenlies. A war was going on. As I watched the news, I
realized that just as America wasn't sure who their enemy was, many in America are
blind to the enemy of their souls, the one who comes to kill, steal and destroy . . .

God is in control and God will ultimately have His way. Let us keep an atti-
tude of prayer, knowing that is where the true battle is won. We gain wisdom on
our knees, power is released on our knees, love pours into our hearts on our knees.

Be assured that God Almighty has roused Himself from His throne. Death will not
have the last say. Immorality will not have the last say. Terrorists will not have the last
say. Destruction will not have the last say. Certainly, evil will not have the last say.

Our God, our Jehovah, our King of kings and Lord of lords, He will most def-
initely have the last say. Every knee will bow and every tongue will confess that
Jesus is Lord. Count on it.

Then, with the same passion, Kathy began to sing "Live for the Lord."
Women poured toward the altar, like a flood, falling on their knees in repentance, pleading with God for His mercy.

Kathy had reminded them of the truth during a time of suffering, pain,
and doubt. Truth is one of the most important colors of His love, breathing
life into our being, like the clear blue skies in the Colorado mountains.

Perhaps her depth and truthfulness come from going through so many
deep waters. Sometimes her bold statements shock, yet they have also been
used to awaken a sleeping church. Usually, she does not just plunge in and hit
people over the head. Kathy is a master at connecting with her audiences,
making them laugh and stirring their souls with song. She's tilling the ground,
preparing hearts to receive the truth. When she senses they are ready, I have
watched her boldly drop seeds of truth that fly in the face of many erroneous
beliefs women have embraced. They listen carefully, as she says:

Prozac is not a dirty word. If you are struggling with depression—good for you
for getting help!

Partial birth abortion is from the pit of hell.

The reason the world embraces spirituality but rejects Christianity is because there is no cost. Christianity demands the cross. We don't want to die.

Those who look to Him are radiant. A beautiful woman is a woman who knows that she is God's beloved.

Don't be afraid to die to yourself. With every cross you pick up, there will be a resurrection!

Kathy is just as honest in private. Once, when I was visiting with one of Kathy's close friends she said, "Kathy speaks the truth over me." I thought, *Yes. That's what she does for us. That's why we are so drawn to her.* I have realized that the women who are my closest friends all have this quality of genuineness. I long for that. I believe Jesus delighted in this characteristic as well, for when He saw Nathanael approaching He said:

Here is a true Israelite, in whom there is nothing false. (John 1:47b)

It is life-giving to be with a person who is authentic, who speaks the truth in love, and who isn't afraid to make themselves vulnerable. It's one of the reasons I have delighted in meditating over the Word of God with Kathy. Often I'll read a passage to her, and, even if she is not extremely familiar with it, she sees it with clear eyes or asks the questions others think but are hesitant to articulate. When I went through the book of Esther with her and showed her the dark passage of Esther 2:12–14, she saw the truth quickly. I remember our conversation so well.

"So, Dee, this says that Esther went to the king in the evening and left in the morning."

"Right."

"And she didn't go back to live with the virgins, but went to live with the concubines."

"Right."

"Because she wasn't a virgin anymore."

"Right."

"Why isn't this emphasized by preachers?"

"Some do. I heard it first from a preacher named John Bronson. I asked a Hebrew scholar at Dallas Theological Seminary if Bronson was right, and she said, "Absolutely." She explained that it's glaringly clear in the Hebrew. The phrase "pleases the king" has a strong sexual innuendo. And the phrase "go into the king" is the same phrase that is used whenever a sexual encounter takes place, such as David 'went into Bathsheba' or Boaz 'went into Ruth.' It's subtle in the English, but it's still clear if you look closely. I think the main reason it isn't emphasized is because we just don't *want* to see it. We want heroes without feet of clay."

"Wow."

"Kath, some people won't like it that we say Esther should not have slept with the king."

She shook her head and smiled. "Well, she shouldn't have, but it's easy to see why she did."

"Yes, some will argue she didn't have a choice—that if Mordecai had refused to let her go, that they might have killed both of them."

"Would they have?"

"Maybe. Xerxes was a cruel king. But they still could have refused the way Shadrach, Meshach, and Abednego refused to bow down to the golden idol. They expected God to deliver them, but they also said, 'Even if He does not we will not bow down.'"

"Well, we have to tell the truth, Dee. It sure takes a great trust to be obedient, especially in circumstances where you might lose your life. I want to have that kind of heart."

I thought she would respond that way. But I still had to warn her.

"There will also be people, Kath, who will say that she was right to sleep with the king because she was then able to save her people from a holocaust."

"If you are going to think that way, you open a whole bucket of worms. That's the kind of thinking that leads women to do all sorts of things. We rationalize without His truth. It's mushy thinking."

"Yes, it is. I just want you to be prepared for some angry letters."

"I know, Dee. I don't like them. But such is life."

I smiled. We high-fived each other.

In the same way, when we looked at 1 John, I remember Kathy's reaction to John's "black-and-white" pronouncements.

"Help! It makes you want to run for the hills."

I laughed. I had *thought* and *felt* that, but would I have dared to say it? *How like Kathy to be so refreshingly honest.* Smiling, I shook my head and said:

"Kathy Troccoli's commentary on 1 John!"

John's statements *are* sobering, for God demands that we stay in the light, die to ourselves, and love our brother. Yet Kathy not only saw the height of God's standards, but the power in them. Passionately, she said:

"This is my heart, Dee, this is what I want to proclaim so women can go higher."

This same spirit of truth and boldness draws me to Bible teacher Jan Silvious. When Jan shares a platform with me I absolutely kidnap her during our off-times and get her take on any difficult situations in my life. Her sane thinking always breathes life into my soul. How often Jan has poured a bucket of cold water over a balmy believer who is twisting a scriptural principle or carrying a burden God never intended her to carry. So often when a person like this calls Jan for advice on the radio, Jan brings her to her senses, by asking a simple question such as:

"Where is it written?"

The caller hesitates, ponders, and then, hopefully, realizes she has been walking in the foolishness of man and not in the power of God. One of Jan's signature books is *Fool-Proofing Your Life,* where she talks about foolishness according to Proverbs. A fool trusts in his own heart, is always right, and uses anger to control. For a fool, everything is always all about him. (Kathy likes to say, "Enough about me. Let's talk about you. What do you think about me?") A fool is the opposite of one who seeks and embraces the truth. The bondage and the destruction in his life, to him and to those close to him, are enormous. The fool embraces the spirit of this world, which *is* the spirit of falsehood. The spirit of falsehood is like the smog of a city, breeding hate, bondage, and death; whereas the spirit of truth is like the clear mountain air, breeding love, freedom, and life. When I ski, I go down the mountain trails leisurely, stopping when I reach a clearing to take a deep breath and look around. It is a spiritual experience to take in the beauty of the snowcapped mountains and the green pine trees against the backdrop of the bluest of skies. How I want to be a woman who is like that clear blue sky, discerning, embracing, and proclaiming the truth. In so doing, I will bring love, freedom, and life.

THE SPIRIT OF FALSEHOOD

This is where the apostle John now turns his attention. He tells us how to tell the difference between the spirit of falsehood and the spirit of truth. Though the world cares nothing for doctrine and measures a Christian's authenticity only on the basis of love, we, as believers, must consider doctrine as well. We must consider the things we hear and measure them against God's plumb line of truth. Even a small deception can distort truth, and also, therefore, love—like a dab of black paint distorts a pint of bold red or bright yellow. What was once pure and lovely is ruined. So it is with the spirit of falsehood.

John explains that the antichrist, the one who will war against Christ, is coming. *Before* he comes, his way is being prepared by "many antichrists," or as theologian John Stott explains, "a spirit of antichrist at work in the world."[1] This spirit is as old as our ancient foe and truly *reigns* in our world today. It's in our movies, our talk shows, our universities, our women's magazines, and in the minds and mouths of those who do not know God. How do we recognize this foolish spirit so that it doesn't pollute our own hearts and souls?

The apostle begins with the key test for falsehood and then elaborates. First John is like a lovely piece of music, beginning with a theme and then building. With rhythmic style, John states his theme simply and then gives variations on it. We've seen him do it with light and darkness, life and death, and now, he does the same with truth and falsehood.

John has been talking about lies and liars from the beginning of his letter, saying we should take note of *behavior*. If we claim to have fellowship with Jesus yet walk in darkness, we lie. If we claim to know Jesus, yet hate our brother, we lie. But now, in the middle of his letter, John switches from behavior to doctrine, and to the *ultimate* lie, the primary test of the spirit of falsehood. What is the *key test* of the spirit of the antichrist? What is the *ultimate lie*?

DENYING CHRIST

John declares it plainly:

> *Who is the liar? It is the man who denies that Jesus is the Christ.* (1 John 2:22a)

It's quite simple, actually, and understanding this test can help you spot the spirit of falsehood when you watch a talk show, read an editorial, or listen to your brother-in-law philosophize at Thanksgiving. What does it mean to "deny Jesus is the Christ"?

Jesus means "Jehovah saves." *Christ* means "the anointed one, the Messiah." *Therefore, the one who denies that Jesus is the Christ is denying the atonement for sin and the true identity of Jesus.* This spirit may call Jesus a teacher or a prophet, but it does not believe He is fully man and fully God. It preaches a different Jesus. Those controlled by this spirit may admit that the world has problems, but the solution of the Scriptures (repentance and faith in Christ) is foolishness to them. Instead they suggest education, money, or "spirituality," but not Christianity. (Doesn't *that* make for much more pleasant dinner conversation?)

They trust in themselves or their own way of defining God, but not in the living Christ.

This spirit of falsehood *is* in the cults and false teachings, which John says, "went out from us, but they did not really belong to us. For if they had belonged to us, they would have remained with us" (1 John 2:19). But it is not only cults or false teachings that twist the identity of Jesus. That would be too easy to identify! *This spirit is the spirit of this age, the spirit that worships man instead of God.* It does not simply ring the bell when a cult member arrives on our doorstep. It flows right into our homes through the river of the mass media. It tries to pollute our hearts through the mouths of well-intentioned but misguided counselors, teachers, and even ministers—and we must be able to recognize it.

Jennifer, a young woman who was trying to overcome a painful past, was going to a woman who claimed to be a Christian counselor. But during one session this counselor told Jennifer that there were many ways to God, and Jesus was just one of those ways. Reflectively, Jennifer said,

> *Though I loved this woman, at that moment I recognized the deception in what I was hearing. I thought, If that were true, why was the Cross necessary? And what about the verse that tells us there is no other name under heaven by which we may be saved? I realized I had been told the "ultimate lie" and I knew I had to change counselors. Only the truth could set me free.*

After establishing the key test, John then augments this theme with another important test.

IT SPEAKS FROM THE VIEWPOINT OF THE WORLD

The spirit of falsehood tolerates all opinions except one. It embraces everything the world believes but rejects the truth of Jesus. This is also how you can discern the spirit of this age. John explains:

> *They are from the world and therefore speak from the viewpoint of the world, and the world listens to them. We are from God, and whoever knows God*

listens to us; but whoever is not from God does not listen to us. This is how we recognize the Spirit of truth and the spirit of falsehood. (1 John 4:5–6)

This spirit was at work in the days of ancient Persia, in the story of Esther. It embraced many ideas, but turned its back on the truth of the God of Israel. The solutions that the Persian leaders sought were the lust of the flesh (through sexual immorality and drunkenness), the lust of the eyes (through the ostentatious display of wealth), and the pride of life (through the plan to invade Greece and add to their territory). This viewpoint also specifically rejected one people: God's people—the Jewish people. This is the people of whom Haman said to Xerxes:

It is not in the king's best interest to tolerate them. (Esther 3:8b)

Today this same spirit of falsehood, though, ironically *preaches* tolerance, yet does not *practice* tolerance toward Christians. It ridicules the viewpoint of the believer in politics, in education, and even in religion. It is the spirit of the antichrist. It listens to every viewpoint except one, and seeks to annihilate *that* viewpoint. And the world listens to that viewpoint, repeating its slogans as if they were the gospel truth. It labels us as "right-wing zealots," "fundamentalist fanatics," or "narrow-minded bigots," hoping to persuade others not to tolerate us. The origins of this spirit are of old. It is our ancient foe.

When God's people are living colorless and flat lives, our enemy curls up for a nap. But when life is breathed into God's people, when the movie turns to Technicolor, he wakes from his slumber. Like a hungry lion the devil prowls, planning his attack, but we have no need to fear, for John reminds us:

The one who is in you is greater than the one who is in the world. (1 John 4:4)

It is vital to understand that this power isn't automatic, but comes and grows through applying the principles of 1 John. Not only do we need to walk in the light and die to ourselves, we *must* continually pour truth into our souls and embrace that truth. If we don't, we will not even recognize the difference between the viewpoint of the world and the viewpoint of God.

SOUL FILLED WITH TRUTH

(Dee) As a young believer I saw dramatic growth in my life when I became serious about pouring the Word of God into my soul. I was frustrated because our firstborn, who was three, was in control of our home. That was the summer I decided I would "master" the book of Proverbs. (Now I realize that's laughable—you couldn't do that in a lifetime!) But every morning, before our little boys awakened, I curled up and meditated on a chapter in Proverbs, read a commentary, and wrote down what I'd learned. I began to discern the difference between the world's viewpoint in raising children and God's viewpoint. I gained strength, wisdom, and effectiveness as a mother. Boundaries were set down and enforced, and our little boy became not only a delight to my soul, but a secure and happy child. Truth was setting us free.

I also formed the habit of meeting with the Lord every day at the same time and the same place with a sense of expectancy that He would speak to me. In my thirty-five years as a believer, I've used many approaches to pour God's truth into myself. If you are doing the accompanying workbook, we will share some of these specific ideas with you.

In Richard Foster's classic, *Celebration of Discipline*, he says: "The desperate need today is not for a greater number of intelligent people, or gifted people, but deep people."² We have been saying the same thing, we don't need "dead women walking," we need vibrant women alive with the truth of God, women who are taking Jesus seriously. We need women who are sowing to please the Spirit rather than the flesh, pouring good things into their souls so that they may see a harvest of righteousness.

Plot your strategy for success. Plan the ways you will immerse yourself in truth. When, daily, could you have your time with God? Do you need the accountability of a small group? When, daily, might you also take some time for reading good books, listening to Christian radio, or to programs over the Internet? How could you make singing to the Lord and listening to music that feeds your soul an integral part of your life? Start sowing to the Spirit and you will be amazed at what the Spirit will produce. The slogan that Nike uses for physical exercise works just as well for spiritual exercise: *Just Do It.*

When you begin to soak in truth, however you do it (and you will discover what methods work best for you), the truth will awaken and empower you.

PAIN IS GOD'S MEGAPHONE

Before the crisis in the book of Esther, the believers (the Jews) had been walking in the ways of the world. It was difficult to tell the difference between them and the citizens of Persia. But the king's edict for their extermination brought them not only to their senses, but also to their knees. They repented, they put on sackcloth and ashes, they fasted and, we assume, therefore, that they prayed, crying out to God for wisdom and truth.

Mordecai led the way. There is no longer any mystery concerning *his* identity. He plopped himself right in front of the palace window in sackcloth and ashes, weeping and wailing. Esther, of course, saw him, and was distressed. She knew he could not come into the palace wearing sackcloth and ashes, so she sent a eunuch with a change of clothes for him.

Mordecai refused the clothes. Instead, he sent a message to Esther. He told her to go to the king and reveal that she was Jewish. Put yourself in her place. Using a contemporary parallel, imagine that you were a young Jewish woman during World War II who had hidden your faith from Hitler and had become his wife. Now, after seven years of deception, you are being told to go and tell him the truth and plead for your people.

Wouldn't you be terrified? Esther certainly was. She expressed her fears in a message to Mordecai. She gave him two good reasons for her refusal:

1. It was against the law. (No one could approach the king without being summoned. If they did, they were to be put to death.)

2. She was unsure of Xerxes feelings for her, for he hadn't called her to his bed in a month.

If you just took Esther at face value and didn't realize the severity of the big picture, you might think,

You know what, Esther? You're exactly right. That all makes sense. You shouldn't go.

Each of us faces times in our lives when, if we have eternity in mind, there is a glaring choice to be made between the path of God and the path of the world. Yet, filled with fear, we rationalize. We dance around to save our own skin. We might not come clean in situations where we have hurt someone; we'll water down our convictions so that we don't look like a "closed-minded Christian"; we'll compromise on the job so that we might be promoted; or we'll fail to speak the truth in love to a friend, so that we don't offend, to the detriment of their spiritual health.

Mordecai didn't let Esther off the hook. Instead he awakened her and made the most famous speech in the book of Esther. He gave her two reasons for doing what is *right*, even though he realized it might mean her death. But these reasons were so filled with truth that her former rational no longer had a say. First, Mordecai warned:

> *Do not think that because you are in the king's house you alone of all the Jews will escape.* (Esther 4:13)

In other words, there is no escape! She can't hide anymore. Mordecai had already revealed his identity, and many knew she was linked to him. Trying to cling to her life at this point was futile.

Do you see the parallel? Jesus said:

> *If you cling to your life, you will lose it; but if you give it up for me, you will save it.* (Matthew 10:39 TLB)

If we are willing to die for what is important to God, there *will* be new life. Not only that, there will be a sense of wellness. Kathy writes in her song, *A Different Road*:

> *Don't want to live without the peace*
> *that comes to me when I am by your side*
> *I've known the freedom there*
> *can't find it anywhere*
> *but in Christ Jesus*[3]

The world passes away, but the person who lives for God stores up treasures that can never pass away. This is what Mordecai was saying. He continued, augmenting his argument to Esther:

> For if you remain silent at this time, relief and deliverance for the Jews will arise from another place, but you and your father's family will perish. (Esther 4:14a)

What Mordecai knew, as every Jew knew, was that God's people were the apple of His eye, and He would *always* have a remnant. If Esther shrank from her responsibility, God would use someone else, somewhere else. The Jews in Persia would be wiped out, and God would move His anointing to someone else. This is sobering. No one is indispensable. It doesn't matter who you are or what you do.

If you will *not* heed the call of God, He will most definitely use someone else. He is looking, the Scripture tells us, for those who are *fully* committed to Him:

> For the eyes of the LORD range throughout the earth to strengthen those whose hearts are fully committed to him. (2 Chronicles 16:9a)

If we are not committed to Him, He will find someone who is. That is Mordecai's point to Esther. Elizabeth Dole said that understanding this truth caused her to want to live a radically obedient life, so that He would use her and not move on to someone else.

Finally Mordecai gave the clincher, the most famous verse in Esther:

> And who knows but that you have come to royal position for such a time as this? (Esther 4:14b)

We do not believe that God led Esther to sleep with the king so that she could one day deliver her people from a holocaust, for God's Spirit never leads against His Word. The Word and the Spirit always confirm one another, are always of like mind. This is a third test that John gives for discerning the spirit of falsehood. (The first was that the spirit of falsehood denies Christ; the second is that it speaks from the viewpoint of the world; and the third is that it contradicts the Word of God.) Since God's Word is clear that we are to refrain from sexual immorality, we know His Spirit did not lead Esther to commit sexual immorality.

However, it is also true that our God is a Master of bringing beauty out of ashes, and that He can redeem our failures. Though Esther (and Mordecai) took the "low road," God still accomplishes His purposes. In His mercy, God gave Esther another opportunity to take the high road. It involved walking in the light, dying to herself, and speaking the truth.

True Blue

Taking the high road means trusting that God "exists and that he rewards those who earnestly seek him" (Hebrews 11:6). Taking action on the basis of this truth is what transforms us into holy women. This is what happens now to Esther. If this were a black-and-white movie, it is at this point that we would change it to living color, for Esther takes a deep breath and says:

> Go, gather together all the Jews who are in Susa, and fast for me. Do not eat or drink for three days, night or day. I and my maids will fast as you do. When this is done, I will go to the king, even though it is against the law. And if I perish, I perish. (Esther 4:16)

There are different kinds of fasts, but a crisis of this magnitude called for a total fast from food and water. During this time God gave Esther enormous wisdom, a plan, courage, and His anointing when she went before Xerxes. She then "puts on her royal robes" and goes to the king. God went before Esther, for Xerxes extended his scepter, the sign of favor.

How wonderful it must have been for Esther to see him extend his scepter and then to hear his words:

> What is it, Queen Esther? What is your request? Even up to half the kingdom, it will be given you. (Esther 5:3)

ENGRAVING OF ESTHER
THE QUEEN

L. CHERON, PAINTER, N. PARR,
ENGRAVER, 1762

Wisely, Esther does not tell him immediately. Instead, she graciously asks if he, along with Haman, could come to a banquet. Then, even at that banquet, she *still* doesn't tell them. She asks for more time by inviting them to yet another banquet the next day.

During the interval, we see God on the move. Let's remember that He does the same for us. We must be patient, trusting Him to work out problems that we have placed in His capable hands. Exodus 14:14 tells us, "The LORD will fight for you; you need only to be still." Many times we want to make a quick phone call, or send off an e-mail to get our point across, but if we would just wait, and pray, we would see God work in the hearts of the people involved. You can read the fascinating story of how He worked in the heart of Xerxes during that time (Esther 5–6). By the time Esther is ready to speak the truth, the king's heart has been prepared, like tilled soil, for the seed of God's truth, for we are told:

So the king and Haman went to dine with Queen Esther, and as they were drinking wine on that second day, the king again asked, "Queen Esther, what is your petition? It will be given you. What is your request? Even up to half the kingdom, it will be granted." (Esther 7:1–2)

No doubt Esther was afraid, but she was also brave, trusting in the Lord. She was gracious, for it is always wise to approach a lion carefully. She said:

If I have found favor with you, O king, and if it pleases your majesty, grant me my life—this is my petition. And spare my people—this is my request. For I and my people have been sold for destruction and slaughter and annihilation. If we had merely been sold as male and female slaves, I would have kept quiet, because no such distress would justify disturbing the king. (Esther 7:3–4)

Do you see the Spirit of God on Esther, giving her wisdom? She has grace under pressure, and she has seized the fact that Xerxes offered her a petition *and* a request. Her reply asks for her life and the lives of her people. She also lets him know that she and her people would have submitted to slavery, but not to death, and that a bribe was involved on the part of the evil party. What is Xerxes' response?

Who is he? Where is the man who has dared to do such a thing? (Esther 7:5)

Esther said,

The adversary and enemy is this vile Haman. (Esther 7:6)

This painting of Xerxes (also known as Ahaseurus) may have been inspired by Proverbs 19:12, which tells us that "a king's rage is like the roar of a lion."

A CONTEMPORARY PARALLEL

(*Dee*) Do you remember the prayer group of mothers I told you about? I am so thankful that Satan was unable to divide us, for when our daughters were

THE WRATH OF
AHASUERUS

JAN STEEN (1626–1679)

seniors in high school, we saw God do amazing things through their friend-ship. They had been seeking God on how to reach their high school for Christ. They decided to follow Esther's example and fast, going without their lunches for a week. They asked God for a plan to reach their peers. Some of the mothers had been studying *Experiencing God*, where it talks about the importance of seeking God and then moving out, rather than coming up with an idea and asking God to bless it. This is what Esther exemplified, and they were going to follow in her steps.

At the end of this particular week they learned that Campus Crusade was bringing the *Jesus* movie to town the week before Easter. They wondered: *Would it be possible to have a private showing for teens?* Campus Crusade quickly agreed—but the challenge was to persuade their principal, Dr. Kenagy. I remember when Sally told me their plan, I thought: *There is no way that is going to happen.* I'll always remember the conversation I had with Sally:

"Mom, we're going to go without lunches for another week. Then we are going to draw straws. Whoever gets the shortest straw will go to Dr. Kenagy and ask if we can have a private showing, announce it over the loudspeaker system, and put the life-size posters of Jesus in the halls."

"Honey, don't get your hopes up. I can't see how Dr. Kenagy will agree to this."

"But Mom, don't you remember how God worked in the heart of Xerxes after Esther and her friends fasted?"

"Yes, but . . ."

"Mom, Dr. Kenagy is a much more reasonable man than Xerxes."

"But this is a public high school—and they are so jittery about Jesus. Remember, the world tolerates everyone except Jesus."

"Mom, isn't this what you have been teaching me? If God is with us, who can be against us? I know Satan is strong, but greater is He who is in us than he who is in the world!"

I was silenced, humbled by my daughter's faith.

I prayed fervently, as did the other mothers. We didn't want our daughters to experience the disappointment of the realities of life. Not everyone is going to welcome Jesus Christ. Not everyone is going to welcome the gospel.

They continued their fast, excitement filling their hearts. On Friday they drew straws.

Sally drew the shortest straw. She went to Dr. Kenagy's office, knocked, and asked if she could have an appointment to speak to him about something important. Innocently Sally wanted to follow Esther's example of allowing God to move in her principal's heart.

"This is a good time for me, Sally. We can talk right now."

"I'd appreciate it so much if I could tell you next Monday, Dr. Kenagy."

"What's this about, Sally?"

"Sir, I would rather wait. Could we do it Monday?"

He raised his eyebrows quizzically, but put her down for Monday at 8 A.M.

That weekend we saw God working behind the scenes. Both Sally and the principal's daughter, Katie, were in a high school singing group called "The Madrigals." All year they had practiced for the state competition to be held that Saturday in Grand Island, Nebraska. Sally had decided to go to Lincoln, which is near Grand Island, to visit her brother and his wife the night before—but she forgot the black dress she needed to sing in the contest. It was hanging in the choir room at school, and by now the school was locked for the weekend.

GOD ON THE MOVE

Sally knew that the principal would have a key to the choir room *and* that he was bringing his daughter Katie to Grand Island in the morning. So Sally called Katie, Katie checked with her dad, and he graciously said, "Sure, I'll pick up Sally's dress." He did, brought it home, and planned to bring it in the morning.

The next morning it was snowing hard. Realizing traffic would be slower than usual, Dr. Kenagy and Katie hurried out the door, leaving Sally's dress hanging on the hook, forgotten.

When they arrived in Grand Island, Sally came running out, saying, "Thank you *so* much for bringing my dress."

The principal and his daughter turned white. Dr. Kenagy said, "Oh no, Sally. I can't believe I forgot it. I am so sorry."

Sally remembers: "Even though I was disappointed, I could also clearly see God's hand. Dr. Kenagy felt *so* badly."

Dr. Kenagy called our home several timess and left messages on the machine apologizing profusely and commenting on Sally's graciousness.

That Monday, when Sally walked into Dr. Kenagy's office, he said: "Whatever you want, Sally, you can have it."

Life-size posters of *Jesus* were hung in the halls of the public high school. Fliers were placed on every car. Several hundred students came and dozens gave their lives to Christ. The girls had Bible studies for beginners already set up, and the discipling process began.

If God be for us, who can be against us?

Principle Four:
Transformed
by Mercy

Have mercy on me, O God, according to your
unfailing love; according to your great compassion . . .
Wash me, and I will be whiter than snow.

(Psalm 51:1, 7)

Clothe yourselves with compassion . . .

(COLOSSIANS 3:12B)

CHAPTER 9

WHITE AS SNOW

Max Lucado helps us imagine the amazing day when Christ will come:

As if the sky were a curtain, the drapes of the atmosphere part. A brilliant light spills onto the earth. There are no shadows. None. From whence came the light begins to tumble a river of color—spiking crystals of every hue ever seen and a million more never seen. Riding on the flow is an endless fleet of angels. They pass through the curtains one myriad at a time until they occupy every square inch of the sky. North. South. East. West. Thousands of silvery wings rise and fall in unison, and over the sound of the trumpets, you can hear the cherubim and seraphim chanting, "Holy, holy, holy."

. . . Suddenly the heavens are quiet. All is quiet. The angels turn, you turn, the entire world turns—and there he is. Jesus.[1]

Max Lucado says that most of us feel discomfort at the thought of this moment, for we know He is holy and we are not. Yet, it is possible, according to John's letter, to prepare for this day. When Jesus sees you, wouldn't you love to see pleasure in His eyes? How can your wedding gown be as white as

171

snow, and embroidered with gold? The refrain of 1 John has been to become like the Lord. How can the imprint be strong in you?

> *Light—Because He is light, we must stay in the light.*
> *Death—Because He laid down His life, we must die to ourselves.*
> *Truth—Because He is truth, we must live by the truth.*

And finally,

> *Mercy—Because He is merciful, we must be merciful.*

John clearly says that as we do all these things, the imprint of the Lord will be visible in us, for His love will be made complete in us. Look at this amazing truth!

> *No one has ever seen God; but if we love one another, God lives in us and his love is made complete in us.* (1 John 4:12)

Henri Nouwen, in studying Rembrandt's painting *The Return of the Prodigal Son,* said that when he first studied this painting, he identified with the sons—first the younger son, and then the elder son. That is what most of us do when we study this famous parable, for we have all been prodigals, wasting God's good gifts like the younger son; and we have all been ungrateful, like the elder son. Nouwen wrote, "It feels somehow good to be able to say: 'These sons are like me.' It gives a sense of being understood."[2] But how does it feel to identify with the father? This is the core, Nouwen says, of the teaching of Christ. This is the multifold secret of being embroidered with the colors of His love. This is the heart of 1 John. As Henri Nouwen stood gazing at Rembrandt's painting, he realized that the real questions we should be asking ourselves are

> *Do I want to be like the father?*
> *Do I want to be not just the one forgiven but the one who forgives?*
> *Do I want to be not just the one welcomed home, but the one who welcomes home?*
> *Do I want to be not just the one who receives compassion, but offers it as well?*

So often the best-selling Christian books, the most treasured sermons, and the whole orientation of the church are about what Christianity can do for us. We are still intent on what the Father can do for us. Instead of being "in this world like him" (1 John 4:17), it's still all about us. But our wedding gowns will never be embroidered with the colors of His love until we can love the way He does. The *final* principle John addresses is mercy, which is shown so clearly in the father in this parable. Nouwen says that the father's mercy consists of:

- Grief (for the brokenhearted)
- Forgiveness (for the transgressor)
- Generosity (for those in need)

Do we remember to love like this on a daily basis?

(Kathy) One day my friend Allyson's son, Logan, was playing with some toys under the kitchen table where Allyson and her sister-in-law, Becky Baker, were having coffee. Aunt Becky is his favorite baby-sitter: sweet, fun, and absolutely devoted to him and his brothers. But that day, the sadness in her voice caught his attention, and he sat Indian-style under the table, listening. Aunt Becky was talking about the man she'd been dating for many months, saying she was now getting mixed signals. Her hopes for a wonderful future were dying. Hearing hurt in his Aunt Becky's voice, Logan emerged from under the table. Putting his little hand on her arm he said:

"Aunt Becky, he's just a 'Love-Forgetter.'"

TALK IS CHEAP

It is so easy, John tells us, to say the words, but to fail to follow through. Isn't it wonderful that we serve a God who is not a Love-Forgetter? John reminds us of His model:

This is how we know what love is: Jesus Christ laid down his life for us.
And we ought to lay down our lives for our brothers. If anyone has material

posessions and sees his brother in need but has no pity on him, how can the love of God be in him? Dear children, let us not love with words or tongue but with actions and in truth. (1 John 3:16–18)

Too often, when we perceive that the cost is going to be higher than we want to pay, we close the door on our hearts, or as the King James Version puts it, we "shutteth up" our compassions (1 John 3:17b KJV).

This is exactly what happened in the book of Esther. Xerxes was smooth with his words, promising much. But when it came time to deliver, Xerxes made good on only *half* of his promise—the part that mattered to him. He made sure Esther was safe by executing Haman. But as far as reversing the edict for the holocaust against the Jews, that was a bit messy. Edicts could not be reversed. Because this was complicated, Xerxes shuts up his compassions. He was a Love-Forgetter.

Esther, in sharp contrast, remembers and follows through. If she had been only trying to save her own life, she would not have gone back, but constrained by love, she returned to plead with Xerxes. Like God the Father, she identifies with her people. She hears their cries of distress. Her heart breaks because their hearts are breaking. Dr. Joyce Baldwin writes:

> *It is very moving to see the extent to which this young girl, who has everything money can buy, identifies herself with her own kith and kin, and is prepared to risk everything to prevent the disaster that threatens them.*[3]

GRIEF FOR THE BROKENHEARTED

Overwhelmed with compassion, Esther returns and passionately pleads for her people. Plainly she tells Xerxes that the second part of the promise is terribly important to *her.* One Hebrew scholar says that her words "if I am pleasing in your eyes," could be interpreted, "if you really care for me . . ."[3] Women, especially, can use this phrase in a manipulative way, but here Esther is using it for the deliverance of her people. Then she says:

> *For how can I bear to see disaster fall on my people? How can I bear to see the destruction of my family?* (Esther 8:6)

ESTHER'S GRIEF

GUSTAVE DIOR (1836–1902)

Each of us who has been delivered from hell can be *so* thankful for that deliverance. But how can the love of God be in us if we are satisfied with our portion and shut up our compassions to those who are still in the dark?

Consider John's phrase "shut up" your compassions. It is a self-protective response. It takes faith to live in a way where your heart always remains open to those in need, believing God will be with you. It takes even more faith when you do not see immediate results, but you must be like Esther and persist, for if you do not, how can the love of God be in you?

DON'T CLOSE DOWN

(Kathy) When my friend Ellie moved from New York to Virginia, she went through severe culture shock. She felt "normal" in New York, where demonstrative Italian women are everywhere, but in Rustin, Virginia, Ellie said, "I talked too fast, was too bold, and my hair was too big." In her book, *Slices of Life,* she tells how intimidated she was by the "blonde women." She writes:

They were not the blonde women from blonde women jokes. My blonde women were smart, sophisticated, articulate, talented, athletic, accessorized, and very thin . . . and those were just some of the reasons I did not like them. They just smiled and nodded and smiled and nodded. I could never tell what they were thinking.[4]

Yet the Lord impressed on her heart that she was to love her neighbor. Ellie argued:

You don't mean right next door—do You, God? Not the blonde women! I'll give to the homeless, I'll visit the prisoner, but do I really have to love the blonde woman? How can I even get to them, Lord? They drive up to their houses, click their garage door opener, and disappear as the door slides down behind them.

God impressed on Ellie's heart that behind the smiles of some of the accessorized blonde women were unfulfilled hearts. He *was* calling her to be His love to them. When she prayed about how to gain credibility with them, she remembered something speaker Daisy Hepburn had told her: "Ellie, you cannot lead people until you first serve them."

"Serving the blonde women took surrender," Ellie said. "It was the beginning of real obedience." Ellie joined the PTA and volunteered at her children's school cafeteria, opening milk cartons and occasionally wiping up vomit. One day in the grocery store an excited little boy went running up to Ellie, recognizing her, tugging on her jacket.

"Mommy, Mommy," he cried to a sophisticated woman dressed in heels and an Ann Taylor suit. "It's the cafeteria lady!" Shaking her head, Ellie said:

It was so humbling for me. I wanted to say, "I had a radio show in New York! I have a master's degree in English! I used to be somebody!" But the Lord quieted me and reminded me of His love. I smiled and talked to her instead about what a great son she had.

Ellie kept serving, kept praying, kept seeking ways to be His love to her neighbors. Finally, like a contemporary Esther, she took the plunge. She walked around her neighborhood, knocking on thirty-three doors, inviting each woman to Bible study. Three came, and Ellie felt *that* was a miracle. The first meeting was low-key and nonthreatening. They laughed through some fun get-acquainted questions, enjoyed good food, and listened attentively as a friend of Ellie's briefly shared how Bible study had changed her life. Ellie reflected:

> *We have something so wonderful to share—we just can't hide it and keep it under a bushel. In New York, when there was a great sale on tomatoes, the Italian women would call and tell each other. Why are we so hesitant to tell people about the secret that leads to eternal life? I told these women: you take care of yourselves physically—you'll go to a gym—you'll take care of yourselves intellectually—you read good books—but you must also take care of yourself spiritually!*

The study Ellie chose was a basic one to introduce them to Jesus. As the weeks passed, excitement began to bubble up—hearts were being softened, eyes opened, and one by one, the women began to place their trust in Christ. John tells us "the whole world is under the control of the evil one" (1 John 5:19), but now those chains were falling off. The truth was setting them free, and their joy was contagious. More neighbors began to come. Ellie said:

> *Who is more fun than new Christians? A whole new world has opened up to them. I remember our first "field trip." They piled into a minivan and we headed to a large Baptist bookstore in Springfield, Virginia. They were astounded—their eye blink rate practically ceased as they walked about in Christian Wonderland: the children's section, the women's section, the music section . . . These women had a lot of spending power. They all bought Bibles, and while their names were being engraved on the covers, they filled their arms with Veggie Tales stuff, t-shirts, books, and tapes.*
>
> *I took the same group to Women of Faith. Same thing. Their jaws hung open as they looked around at 18,000 women singing praises to Jesus. Unless they were at a piano bar, they hadn't sung in years—and now they were singing their hearts out to Jesus!*

Ellie continues to have outreach coffees at Christmas, Valentine's Day, or to celebrate back-to-school for the kids. Today there are fifty-two women in that study and their space and childcare needs have caused them to move the study to a nearby church.

The fields are ripe for harvest. How can we shut up our compassions?

(Dee) In my city, as is true in every American city that has a college, we have many international students. Our college places advertisements like this in overseas newspapers:

> *Apply to the University of Nebraska in Kearney!*
> *Get an excellent and inexpensive American education in a safe small town.*

Each year hundreds of students from Japan, Africa, India, and other far-away places respond. This mission field exists nearly every place there is a college, but American believers so often ignore it. These are the students who are the leaders in their countries, who have traveled to us, who have learned our language, and who are eager for our friendship. Yet, 75 percent of them are never invited into an American home.

An adventure in my life involved Hari, a dynamic young man from Nepal. Hari had put his trust in Christ before we met him, but his nineteen-year-old bride had not. Rita was terribly homesick—missing her mother and father, language, warm climate, and Nepalese food. One day our pastor came to the house with Hari, asking if I would consider having Hari and Rita move in with us, at least until Rita adjusted to America and learned English. "She needs a mother here," our pastor said, his eyes pleading with me. "And our brother here," he said, nodding to Hari, "needs some help." Our pastor knew that Steve and I had been blessed with a large home, and that our two oldest children had moved out, leaving the downstairs, with a bed and bath, vacant. This verse came to me:

> *If anyone has material possessions and sees his brother in need but has no pity*
> *on him, how can the love of God be in him?* (1 John 3:17)

I struggled, as I often have in the past, with my own agenda. But I also was learning to trust the heart of Jesus, and to be open to His Spirit. I agreed to pray and let them know. I asked God to open my heart if this was His calling for me or to release me if it was not.

My heart began to turn toward this couple, and toward Rita, who was only a few years older than our own daughter, Sally. *How would I feel,* I thought, *if Sally were in a faraway land and homesick. Wouldn't I want a woman who loves Jesus to take her under her wing?*

Hari and Rita moved in. Rita immediately called me "Auntie," and Sally, "Sister." One of Hari's first requests was of Sally. He wanted her to help Rita shave her legs, which had never seen the blade of a razor. "Make her smooth," he asked, "like American women." Sally led a wide-eyed Rita into the bathroom, armed with shaving cream and a pink Lady Gillette. For more than an hour we heard shrieks and laughter over the sound of running water. When they emerged, Sally was drenched in perspiration and Rita was wreathed in smiles. She placed first one leg and then the other on a chair, taking my hand and running it over her smooth skin. It was a sweet moment to see her face so full of pleasure.

Another time we took Rita to our cabin in Wisconsin, where she was going to try swimming for the first time. We gave her a suit and she disappeared into the bedroom. When she came out, she had it on backward, with her breasts exposed, hanging freely. My girls clapped their hands over their mouths in astonishment. When Rita understood her mistake, we all collapsed on the floor in laughter.

Because Rita was just learning English, we used Bible picture books for children for our devotional times, trying to introduce her to Jesus. We acted out stories, just as we had done when our children were small, of Jesus calming the storm and healing the lepers. But somehow, the veil seemed to remain over Rita's eyes. She saw Jesus as an American God, and planned to worship Buddha when she and Hari returned to Nepal. I have to admit I was discouraged. Yet I also knew I had responded with an open heart toward Rita. As always, the Holy Spirit would do the rest.

Eventually Hari and Rita moved into their own apartment and began their family. When Rita was pregnant with their second child, she became very ill. The doctor attributed it to a difficult pregnancy. But I'll never forget the phone call from the doctor telling us that further tests revealed that Rita was dying of cancer. Would Steve and I break the news to them?

Though we prayed desperately for healing, it was not to be on this earth. Rita gave birth to their son, Andrew, but had only months to live. My last visit to Rita will live forever in my memory. Rita was on the couch, wrapped in blankets, pale and weak, yet her face lit up when I came through the door. "Auntie!"

I told her not to talk, that I would just sit there with her, but Rita had something she had to tell me. She said, "Auntie, because of this . . . I see who Jesus is now." She told me how He had brought her His peace in the midst of her storm. Together, despite the tremendous sorrow, we wept tears of joy. I told Rita that I was praying she would not die. She had always seemed so childlike to me, but at that very moment, she became like a woman who had known Jesus for years, glimpsing a vision into the heavenlies:

"Auntie, Jesus is calling me home. He has shown me His glory. But Auntie, I need your help."

"Anything, Rita."

"Hari and I need you to find him a wife and a mother who will really love Angela and Andrew and teach them all about Jesus. Will you?"

I hesitated. Could I say a definite yes to this? But how could I not? Suddenly I was sobbing and promising.

Hari took Rita home to be with her parents in her final days. After her death he called me from Nepal, saying simply, "I desperately *need* a wife and a mother for my children." I told him I was praying and then we prayed together on the phone.

I remember the moment when Hari and his children came into my mind as I encountered Christy at a Bible study. I had been impressed with her deep love for the Lord. But the lightbulb moment came when she told me: "I am *so* excited about my plans for spring break." I thought she was going to tell me about a mission trip, or a ski trip, but instead she said, "I'm going to take care of my friend's children while they go away for a week. I'm counting the days."

I remember asking the Lord, *Could she be the one?*

When I told Hari about Christy, he asked me to set up ten dates with her. I had to hold back my laughter. I said, "Hari, that's not how we do it in America. If Christy agrees, I'll set you up for the first date, and we'll pray that if God is in it, that she will agree to see you again."

God had gone before Hari and Christy. They fell deeply in love, but even though they were older, and the need was great, they didn't rush. The children bonded with Christy, and it gave me joy to see them run into her arms whenever they saw her.

A year later Hari and Christy were married at a beautiful ceremony, where Angela was the flower girl and Andrew the ring bearer. Today I absolutely marvel at what God has done. Because the children had been through so much trauma, they were out-of-control toddlers. But today they are happy and well behaved. They know God's Word and they love not only one another, but their new baby sister as well. Christy is the wife and mother for whom Rita and I prayed, for our God is a God who answers prayer.

I had *no* idea when I invited Hari and Rita to live with us what the future held, but God did. All He asks of us is to be available and to keep our hearts open. If we ask Him to break our hearts with the things that break *His* heart, we *will* become actively involved in showing compassion.

FIGHTING TO FORGIVE

When we have been genuinely hurt, it is not *natural* to forgive. Forgive that mother-in-law, neighbor, or friend for what she said? Why, her words cut to the heart! No, the natural response is to want to make her *pay*. But if we are going to be "like Him in this world" we must forgive. We must let the offense go. In sign language the motion for forgive is to take the fingertips of one hand and brush them across the open palm of the other hand in an outward direction, away from yourself, wiping the offense away.

How can we possibly do this? Only by His Spirit, only by His grace. It is vital that we focus not on the offense but on how we have been forgiven, how the merciful Father washed us and made us as white as snow, remembering our sin no more. The portrait of the father in the parable of the prodigal son shows us the three manifestations of mercy:

1. The father felt grief for the brokenhearted:

   But while he was still a long way off, his father saw him and was filled with compassion for him . . . (Luke 15:20b)

2. The father gave forgiveness to the transgressor, even before he heard the son's words of repentance:

   He ran to his son, threw his arms around him and kissed him. (Luke 15:20c)

3. The father was generous to the one in need:

   But the father said to his servants, "Quick! Bring the best robe and put it on him. Put a ring on his finger and sandals on his feet. Bring the fattened calf and kill it. Let's have a feast and celebrate." (Luke 15:22–23)

LIVING OUT MERCY

As we were going through the edit of the manuscript for this book, our editor, Wendy, was profoundly impacted by the principles of 1 John. Married for fifteen years, Wendy became a Christian about eight years ago. Her husband, John, didn't know God. She confessed to us that as she was editing the book, the passages dealing with counterfeit repentance were convicting her of something. She said:

Hey—they're talking to me. I realized that there were times when my submission was counterfeit, and even, in a sense, my love. I may have appeared like a good Christian wife, but there were so many ways I had been selfish. I began to fully repent of my failings and to pray more fervently for God to not only save my husband, but to transform me.

Shortly after that, Wendy and her husband came to a crisis point in their marriage, as she discovered that not only had she failed as a wife, but John had failed her profoundly as a husband. Yet the Spirit of God told Wendy that He wanted her to forgive as He had forgiven her. She was to play the father in the story of the prodigal son and open wide her arms. Only this was no parable. She needed to become like the father for real, and quickly.

> *I knew the Spirit of God was urging me to truly forgive John. I couldn't do it in my own strength, but Christ did it through me. It was like a taste of having my faith perfected. It became clear to my husband, who at the time still did not believe in Jesus, that there was only one reason I was able to forgive him. That reason was Christ living in me.*

We are always to forgive. The Scripture is clear. However, trust is a separate issue. How do we know when to also trust? David provides a model. He forgave Saul from his heart, and he trusted him, until Saul showed a *pattern* of betrayal. Time will reveal if repentance is genuine or counterfeit. When Saul started throwing spears at David for the third time, David continued to forgive, but no longer trusted Saul. He fled for his life. You can forgive someone and yet still be justified in putting space between the two of you. There have been times when we have counseled women to separate from their husbands, for their physical or emotional preservation, until their husbands get help and show the fruit of genuine repentance.

Our editor chose both to forgive *and* to trust her husband, because he showed every evidence of genuine repentance. Broken before God, he met with a godly older man who challenged him to read the Gospel of John. Soon after this John put his trust in Jesus. Now he is hungry for God's Word and overflowing in gratitude to both God and Wendy for their forgiveness. God has truly done a miracle. John testifies to his changed life:

> *Before, life was like a charcoal drawing, but now, it is like a watercolor painting, alive with beautiful colors.*

As a result of this profound forgiveness experience Wendy says God birthed a love and compassion for John in *her heart* that had not been there before in all their fifteen years of marriage. "Give, and it will be given to you. A good measure, pressed down . . . running over . . ." (Luke 6:38).

Forgiveness is an act of grace—something we do because of the great forgiveness we have been given. Malice, which is the opposite of forgiveness, is rampant in the world. John helps us to understand why we do not bear the mark of a Christian when we hate our *brother*. Because our brother and sister have Christ living within them, when we bear malice toward them, we are actually bearing malice toward Jesus.

Remember what John told us in the beginning: either our father is God, or he is the evil one. Cain, whose father was the evil one, hated his brother. Why? John tells us: "Because his own actions were evil and his brother's were righteous" (1 John 3:12). John Stott explains:

> *Cain was the prototype of the world, which manifests the ugly qualities he first displayed . . . It is not just hatred, but hatred of Christian people, which reveals the world in its true colours, for in their persecution of the Church, their antagonism to Christ is concealed.*[5]

When Haman, in the book of Esther, persecuted the believers, it was really a concealed hatred of God. God has high standards, and if an individual does not want to give up going his own way, he is going to hate God and hate those who follow Him. John tells us:

> *Do not be surprised, my brothers, if the world hates you.* (1 John 3:13)

Sometimes Christians pay a high price for their faith, for their light makes a spouse, sibling, friend, or parent who has chosen the dark very uncomfortable. The sword that Jesus predicted would divide brother and sister, husband and wife, and father and child cuts deeply and the severing is painful. But if *we*, who are believers, hate our brother, how can the love of God be in us? Dr. Stott asks us to consider the contrast between a child of the evil one and a child of God.

> *Hate is negative, seeks the other person's harm, and leads to activity against him, even to the point of murder.*

Isn't that what we saw in Cain? He plotted evil against Abel, rose up against him, and murdered him. In contrast, Dr. Stott says:

> *Love is positive, seeks the other person's good, and leads to activity for him, even to the point of self-sacrifice.*[6]

Isn't that what we saw in Esther? She prayed and planned for good for her brethren, rose up, and actively helped them, even to the point of self-sacrifice. This behavior is the evidence that we have passed from death to life.

GENEROSITY

We show the mercy of the Father through grief, forgiveness, and finally, through generosity. We must love not only with words, but also with actions. James makes the same point John does, but with humor:

> *Suppose a brother or sister is without clothes and daily food. If one of you says to him, "Go, I wish you well; keep warm and well fed," but does nothing about his physical needs, what good is it?* (James 2:15–16)

There are *so* many needs in the world, it would be easy to be so overwhelmed that you end up doing *nothing*. But each of us is called to do *something*. God brings people into our lives and puts them on our minds on a regular basis. We must remain sensitive or we will miss seeing the people God is bringing directly to us. It is to these people that we must be generous, seeking ways to be His love to them.

(Dee) When Kathy and I were filming our video for *Falling in Love with Jesus*, a beautiful young woman named Tina came and greeted Kathy like an old friend.

"Do you know her?" I asked when we were alone.

"This is the second time I've met her face-to-face, but I've been sending her flowers for a few years."

"What's the story behind that?"

"She was raped a few years ago, in a shopping mall. When I heard about it, my heart just went out to her. I wanted her to know she was precious and valuable. The Lord put it in my heart to send her occasional floral arrangements and cards to remind her that she was His Beloved."

I love this simple story because it is an example of seeing a need in your sister, planning good for them in whatever way you can, and following through. God gives us opportunities to do this daily, and as we obey, an amazing thing happens. Our confidence that we belong to the truth grows and His Spirit embroiders the colors of His love throughout our "wedding gown." John explains:

> *In this way, love is made complete among us so that we will have confidence on the day of judgment, because in this world we are like him.* (1 John 4:17)

WHITE AS SNOW

(Dee) Kathy was telling me about her friend, Claudette Rondanelli, who had been a drug addict, a topless dancer, and in her own words, "had a mouth like a truckdriver and dressed like a prostitute." God not only brought Claudette into relationship with Him, but she is becoming a radiant woman, because she is learning to walk in the principles of 1 John. Though her sins were as scarlet, today she glistens like the new fallen snow.

When I interviewed Claudette, she told me that when she had first met Kathy, she was not interested in talking to her.

"Why not?" I asked.

> *Kathy was a born-again Christian. I didn't like born-again people. Every one I met was a hypocrite and very mean. Not only that, she was famous. That was like two things against her. I just didn't want nothin' to do with her.*

Claudette's sister-in-law, Dorothy, was a friend of Kathy's. Dorothy played piano in a band at bars on Long Island. Claudette would often go to watch the band. Claudette said:

"Kathy would come and see my sister-in-law play. I'd be drinking, a little toasted, and she'd come over and say, 'How you doing, Claudette, so good to see you.' She was always consistent. She was always loving."

(Kathy) The first time I met Claudette I was a little intimidated by her. She had deep, dark eyes and long, thick, dark hair and a constant cigarette in her mouth. She definitely looked like a "rock-and-roll chick." But despite the fact that she didn't have a warmth or an openness in communication, God just gave me a heart for her. Whenever I would see her, I thought, *I just need to love this girl.* So often we demand people to make a change before we show them the love of Christ. We want the world to act like Christians before they even know Christ. (Acting like Christians is not necessarily a good thing—*acting like Jesus* is a good thing.) We want the alcoholic to lay down his drink long enough so we can pontificate about our beliefs. We want the single mother with three kids to immediately come to church on Sunday even though she works fifty hours a week. We can imagine countless scenarios.

When I first decided to follow Jesus, He didn't say: "Now Kathy, before we start a relationship here, just do Me a favor. Stop being so angry. Stop abusing laxatives. Lose some weight. Don't fight with your mother so much." Can you imagine? And we can all come up with our own list of how God found us. Jesus doesn't require us to give up our gods and our addictions until we truly meet Him and know what we're giving them up for—that's when He wants us to get serious about it. We need to love people just as they are because that's how Jesus loved us.

(Dee) Kathy's loving attitude toward Claudette reminds me of the opening of 1 John, when he expresses his longing for his readers to know the same intimacy with God that he and the other disciples have experienced. That longing to share His love with others is evidence of the reality of God in us. Claudette could see that love in Kathy:

Kathy was always really warm and would ask me about my life, about my kid. I wasn't that eager to talk to her, and I was a little standoffish, but she'd sit down and just keep asking me about myself.

One night I went to her house with Dorothy. Dorothy cooked and Kathy just talked to me. My back hurt and she came around my chair and gently rubbed my shoulders. After a while I started asking her a few questions. She was able to express her heart without condemnation—and she didn't talk to me about any of my "stuff." She just talked to me about Jesus. She talked about Him like He was her husband. He was so real to her. She was so in love with Him. I thought . . . I want that.

Again, I think that the most powerful way to draw both unbelievers and believers closer to the Lord is to allow them to see our own relationship with Jesus. We can only take people to the well we are drinking from. We can fake our love and our faith, but people, and surely God, will know if we aren't real:

What I loved about Kathy was that she was human. There are a lot of Christians who walk around and pretend that they come to Jesus and everything's fine. But I'd see Kathy cry, or get bummed out. She was normal. Some Christians put on a front and you think, Something's wrong here. *Kathy was real, but Jesus' love was in her. That's what drew me. I was starting to open up, asking her anything I wanted.*

One day she said, "Claudette, it sounds like you want to know more. Why don't you come to church with me?"

I said, "Yeah, yeah, okay." I didn't, though, and when she'd see me, she'd mention it again. Finally I promised.

That next Saturday night I went out with my boss and got very high because we went to a wedding. I woke up with a hangover but I thought, You know, I made a promise. *So I went with Kathy and Dorothy.*

I saw everyone singing and praying. I told them, "I'm not going to sing, I'm not going to do anything. I'm just going to sit here."

They said, "You can do whatever you want."

So I sat there and started getting touched by the Holy Spirit. I didn't know that at the time, I was just reading the words of the songs off the screen. There was such a lump in my throat, like a watermelon. I was gasping for air. I leaned over and said, "What's going on here? I feel like I'm going to choke."

Immediately they responded: "Oh, that's the Holy Spirit."

The next week I went back with them. When we were walking into church we were talking about some stuff from the Bible. It nearly knocked me over when the pastor's sermon was on the same stuff. Afterward I told him about that and he said, "Isn't God good?"

I said, "Well . . . yeah . . ."

Then he asked me if I had received Jesus as my personal Savior and Lord. I told him, "No."

He said, "Why not?"

I said, "I'm afraid."

But that was the day I did.

"Love drives out fear" (1 John 4:18). The transformation was beginning in Claudette.

The next day I was running around trying to find a Bible. I'm like, "I can't find a Bible. Are there places around to get Bibles?" So Kathy bought me The Living Bible. *I started reading and God started working in my life very quickly.*

Though Claudette did not know the principles in 1 John, the Holy Spirit was leading her in them. He was drawing her to the light, and drawing her to die to her old way of life:

Some of my stuff went away right away—like my foul mouth. I changed the way I dressed. My husband said, "Where's the sexy woman I married?"

I said, "She's become a lady."

Other stuff took a long time—like my smoking. For thirty years I'd had a pack a day. I couldn't seem to stop. But two years ago I asked God to make me hate it, and I got a terrible upper respiratory infection. That did it.

As Claudette was dying to the old, there was room for the new. Like crocuses that surprise you, pushing through the frozen, snow-covered ground, Claudette's spirit was coming to life. She developed a real love for the Bible, and as she poured truth into her soul, the flowers were spreading in wondrous profusion. The fourth principle, that of showing mercy, began to take hold in her life—something that amazed her.

I really want to be a praying and loving mother and grandmother. One of the biggest things was that I really didn't like people before—and I didn't have time for kids. But now I work in a special-education school. So many in my family have come to Christ. My mom is just sixteen years older than me and now she loves Jesus too. I work in a ministry for Long Island Citizens for Community Values. It's a ministry to help people who have been sexually violated.

(Kathy) Claudette has a great big heart and has blessed me so much. Last year I asked her to come to my New Year's Party. It's my big party every year, and it's become a tradition that my guests participate in a talent show. Some of the "acts" are funny, and some of them are serious. Claudette had been learning sign language and had learned to do it with my song "Lord, I Need You Now" from my very first recording, *Stubborn Love*. So I asked her if she would do it that night for my party. I watched in awe as Claudette tenderly expressed a prayer I sang way back in 1982 before my guests. I just started to cry because I thought, *Dear God, You do make beauty out of ashes.*

All Glorious Is the Princess Within Her Chamber

Do you remember how in the beginning we said that John's "black-and-white" statements could make you want to run for the hills? Now we see that, instead of a negative, these principles are a tremendous positive. They make you want to run to Jesus. As we walk in the light, His light shines more brightly in us. As we die to ourselves, His life springs up in us. As we embrace and speak the truth, the smog lifts from our souls. As we show mercy to our brother and sister, His love "is made complete in us." As we do all these things, our confidence that we belong to the truth grows, setting "our hearts at rest in his presence whenever our hearts condemn us" (1 John 3:19b–20a). We bear the imprint of Christ; we are like Him in this world.

We are now in a period of separation. Our Bridegroom has gone away. In His absence, He pleads with us to obey the principles He gave to John. Jesus *will* be back. If we do these things in His absence, His Spirit will embroider our wedding gown with threads of gold: our intimacy with the Lord will increase, our fellowship with one another will be sweeter, and there will be a *fullness* of joy in our lives. One day a trumpet will sound, and our Bridegroom will appear. We will be radiant brides. Splendid, virtuous, lovely. His cherished princesses. Our gowns will be interwoven with the colors of His love, and in glorious array, we will be led to the King.

NOTES

CHAPTER 1: THE IMPRINT OF A CHRISTIAN

1. James C. Humes and Richard M. Nixon, *The Wit and Wisdom of Winston Churchill: A Treasury of More Than 1,000 Quotations and Anecdotes* (New York: HarperPerennial, 1995), 215.

2. Dee Brestin, *The Friendships of Women* (Colorado Springs: Chariot Victor, 1988), 23.

3. Francis A. Schaeffer, *The Mark of a Christian* (Downers Grove: InterVarsity, 1971), 133.

CHAPTER 3: EMBROIDERED WITH GOLD

1. Charles Spurgeon, *The Comprehensive Spurgeon Collection* [CD-ROM] (Ages Software, 2001), First sermon on John 2:12.

2. Oswald Chambers, *My Utmost for His Highest, An Updated Edition in Today's Language,* ed. James Reiman (Grand Rapids: Discovery House Publishers, 1992), August 13.

3. Charles Spurgeon, *Spurgeon's Expository Encyclopedia, Vol. 10* (Grand Rapids: Baker Books, 1996), 377.

CHAPTER 4: WALKING IN THE DARK

1. Elisabeth Fishel, *Sisters* (New York: Quill, 1979), 1.

2. Dallas Willard, *The Divine Conspiracy* (San Fransisco: HarperCollins, 1998), 1.

3. Lyrics by Kathy Troccoli. Copyright © 1998 Sony/ATV Songs LLC. All rights on behalf of Sony/ATV Songs LLC administered by Sony/ATV Music Publishing, 8 Music Square West, Nashville, TN 37203. All rights reserved. Used by permission.

4. Henri Nouwen, *The Return of the Prodigal* (New York: Doubleday, 1994), 4.

5. Ibid., 98–99.

CHAPTER 5: WALKING IN THE LIGHT

1. Chambers, *My Utmost for His Highest.* Nov. 19.

CHAPTER 6: AUTUMN GLORY

1. John Piper, *Desiring God,* (Sisters: Multnomah Books, 1996), 284.

CHAPTER 7: IT'S NOT EASY BEING GREEN

1. John MacArthur, *The MacArthur Study Bible* (Nashville: W Publishing Group, 1997), 682.

2. F. B. Huey, *The Expositor's Commentary, Vol. 4,* ed. Frank E. Gaebelein and Richard P. Polcyn (Grand Rapids: Zondervan, 1988), 793.

3. MacArthur, *The MacArthur Study Bible*, 682.

4. John F. Brug, *People's Commentary Bible, Ezra-Nehemiah-Esther* (St. Louis: Concordia, 1985), 155–56.

5. Herodotus, *Histories* (New York: Penguin, 1996), 459.

6. Flavius Josephus, *"The Antiquities of the Jews," Josephus: Complete Works,* trans. William Whiston (Grand Rapids: Kregel Publications, 1981), 237.

7. Joyce Baldwin, *"Esther," Tyndale Old Testament Commentary, Vol. 3* (Wheaton: Tyndale, 1984), 48.

8. Josephus, *"The Antiquities of the Jews,"* 35.

9. Joyce Baldwin, *Esther: An Introduction and Commentary* (Downers Grove: IVP, 1984), 66.

10. Carl Armerding, *Esther, For Such Times As This* (Chicago: Moody, 1995), 40.

11. Frederic Bush, *Word Biblical Commentary, Vol. 9* (Dallas: Word Books, 1996), 385.

12. Baldwin, *Esther, Tyndale Old Testament Commentary*, 76.

CHAPTER 8: TRUE BLUE

1. John R.W. Stott, *The Epistles of John* (Grand Rapids: Eerdmans, 1983), 104.

2. Richard Foster, *Celebration of Discipline* (San Francisco: Harper and Row, 1978), 1.

3. Lyrics by Kathy Troccoli. Copyright © 1998 Sony/ATV Songs LLC. All rights on behalf of Sony/ATV Songs LLC administered by Sony/ATV Music Publishing, 8 Music Square West, Nashville, TN 37203. All rights reserved. Used by permission.

CHAPTER 9: WHITE AS SNOW

1. Max Lucado, *When Christ Comes* (Nashville: Word Publishing, 1999), xv, xvi.

2. Henri Nouwen, *The Return of the Prodigal* (New York: Doubleday, 1994), 122.

3. Baldwin, *Esther, Tyndale Old Testament Commentary,* 95.

4. Ellie Lofaro, *Slices of Life: Unexpected Blessings from Real Relationships* (Colorado Springs, Colorado: David C. Cook Publishing Company, 2002), 13.

5. John R.W. Stott, *The Epistles of John* (Grand Rapids: Eerdmans, 1983), 141.

6. Ibid., 142.